Mountain Biking in
Slovenia

About the Author

Rob Houghton has been an outdoor instructor, leader and educator for more years than he cares to count and he has led expeditions on five continents.

Rob has also been a cyclist for as long as he can remember. His first bike was a Raleigh Striker, back when they had fake suspension forks on the front. He was taught to ride by his father who, back in the 1960s, built a front suspension, off-road bike from parts he found in a skip and who, therefore, should have had the rightful claim to having invented mountain bikes a decade before the boys in Marin county.

Rob himself only took up mountain biking 10 years ago after a friend first took him around a trail centre in Wales. He was hooked. Since then he has tried to make up for lost time and has ridden in destinations as diverse as Wales and Thailand, Denmark and Singapore. He has ridden extensively in Slovenia and has spent a great many years visiting the country after spending a year working there in his youth. He even got married in Slovenia but was not allowed to do any riding in the run-up to the celebration.

Among his collection of bikes, Rob still has his first mountain bike, a Voodoo Hoodoo (one of the originals), which has lived in more countries than many people have (five at current count). It now lives in Melbourne where its owner also resides with his very understanding wife Jess.

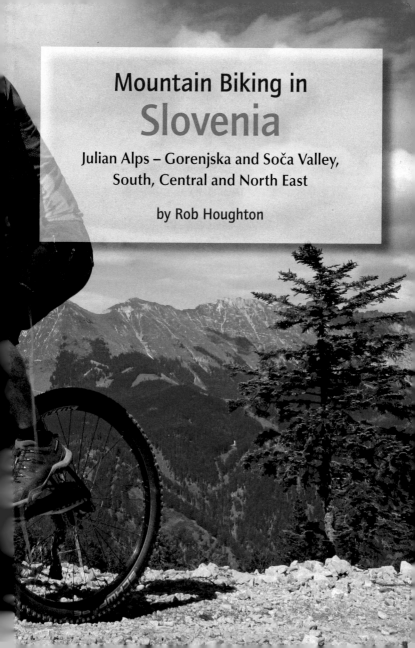

Mountain Biking in
Slovenia

Julian Alps – Gorenjska and Soča Valley, South, Central and North East

by Rob Houghton

© Rob Houghton 2017
First edition 2017
ISBN-13: 978 1 85284 808 8

Printed in China on behalf
of Latitude Press Ltd

© **KARTO**GRAFIJA
www.kartografija.si

Mapping © Kartografija
d.o.o. Ljubljana, Slovenia

All photographs are by the author unless
otherwise stated.

UPDATES TO THIS GUIDE

While every effort is made by our authors
to ensure the accuracy of guidebooks
as they go to print, changes can occur
during the lifetime of an edition. Any
updates that we know of for this guide
will be on the Cicerone website (www.
cicerone.co.uk/808/updates), so please
check before planning your trip. We also
advise that you check information about
such things as transport, accommodation
and shops locally. Even rights of way
can be altered over time. We are always
grateful for information about any
discrepancies between a guidebook and
the facts on the ground, sent by email to
updates@cicerone.co.uk or by post to
Cicerone, 2 Police Square, Milnthorpe
LA7 7PY, United Kingdom.

ACKNOWLEDGEMENTS

I have so many people to thank for
their help in writing this book. First
and foremost, however, is my wife
Jess, without whose encouragement,
emotional support and financial aid,
this book could never have got off the
ground.

Thank you also to all the people
who showed me around. Gregor, Nina,
Bostjan, Jani and Peter all gave me a
local's view on the best trails. They've
also given you someone else, other than
me, to look at in the photos.

The local business community in
Slovenia also jumped to my assistance.
Thanks to Apartma Mavrič, Hotel Golte,
Terme Krka, Hostel Pod Voglem, Hotel
Plesnik, Hotel Lek and Gregor and Nina
(again) for offering me free or heavily
discounted accommodation.

Finally, thanks also to Lucijan at
Proloco who, without knowing me from
Adam, lent me a new Scott bike every
time I came begging. Over 1750km
covered on those borrowed bikes.

*Front cover: Spectacular views topping
out on Stol (Route 10)*

Half title: Descending towards the church
of St Jacob (Route 34)

Title page: Great views if you have the
energy to look (Route 5)

Contents

THE SOUTH   103

CENTRAL AND NORTH EAST   155

APPENDICES

Emergencies

Always carry a charged mobile phone with you so that emergency services can be alerted in case of serious injury.

If you do need to report such an injury, first make a note of all relevant details including location (giving the grid reference if possible), the nature of the injury and your mobile phone number. Then call 112 and ask for both police and ambulance.

Be ready to give the location and nature of the incident and the numbers of any phones carried by the party. Do not change your position until you are contacted by the emergency services.

The contact details of local accident and emergency departments are listed in Appendix C.

For more information, see the Emergency situations section in the introduction.

SYMBOLS USED ON MAPS

~●❶ route/stage number

🛵➜ start/finish point

➜ direction of main route

0 kilometres 0.5 1
0 miles 0.5   SCALE: 1:50,000

🅟 petrol station

🅿 parking area

≋ beach

🏛 spa

▣ swimming pool

❋ ski area

🏛 museum

☒ archaeological site

🔺 mountain hut

🅷 hotel

🍴 inn

DIFFICULTY GRADES

■ medium

▲ hard

◆ very hard

🍴 inn with lodgings

🅱 lodgings

🍴 tourist farm (with lodging)

🍴 excursion farm (without lodging)

🅰 camping

🅲 golf course

⊕ ambulance

🏛 interesting castle

🔆 interesting church

☀ viewpoint

✹ natural feature of interest

Route summary table

Route no.	Route title	Start/Finish	Distance
Gorenjska			
1	The high alpine at Uskovnica	Bohinjska Bistrica	33.75km (21 miles)
2	In the foothills of Črna Prst	Bohinjska Bistrica	26.5km (16½ miles)
3	Across the Jelovica Plateau	Kamna Gorica	38km (23½ miles)
4	To the Crone's Tooth	Kamna Gorica	35.5km (22 miles)
5	Grahovše circular	Grahovše	21.75km (13½ miles)
6	Lake Zgornje	Zgornje Jezersko	13.5km (8½ miles)
7	Peč and the three borders	Kranjska Gora	25.5km (15¾ miles)
8	Kranjska Gora circular	Kranjska Gora	27km (16¾ miles)
The Soča Valley			
9	Kobarid and the River Soča	Kobarid	18.5km (11½ miles)
10	Stol epic	Kobarid	59km (36½ miles)
11	Kobarid and the River Nadiža	Kobarid	14.5km (9 miles)
12	Stol and the long descent	Hotel Ana	37km (23 miles)
13	Planina Razor	Zatolmin	35km (21¾ miles)
14	Most na Soči Široko	Most na Soči	12km (7½ miles)
15	The war memorial at Trnovo	Lokve	22km (13½ miles)
16	The dark forests of Trnovo	Mala Lazna	29km (18 miles)
The South			
17	The industrial heritage of Črni Vrh	Črni Vrh	48km (30 miles)

% OFF ROAD	Ascent	Grade	Time	Time of year
75	1380m (4530ft)	▲	3–4hr	Late spring to early autumn
75	1130m (3705ft)	▲	2–3hr	Spring to autumn
70	1570m (5150ft)	▲	3–4hr	Spring to autumn
85	1315m (4315ft)	◆	3–4hr	Spring to autumn
95	1355m (3725ft)	■	2–2hr 30min	Spring to autumn
70	380m (1245ft)	■	30min–1hr	All year
60	1050m (3445ft)	■	2–3hr	Late spring to early autumn
65	1405m (4610ft)	▲	1hr 30min–2hr 30min	Late spring to early autumn
35	755m (2475ft)	▲	1hr 30min–2hr	Spring to autumn
65	2205m (7235ft)	◆	5–6hr	Late spring to early autumn
65	325m (1065ft)	■	1hr 30min–2hr	All year
75	1660m (5445ft)	◆	4–5hr	Late spring to early autumn
35	2100m (6890ft)	▲	4–5hr	Late spring to early autumn
40	720m (2360ft)	▲/◆	1–1hr 30min	All year
55	350m (1150ft)	■	1hr 30min–2hr	Spring to autumn
90	925m (3035ft)	■	2–3hr	Late spring to early autumn
70	1915m (6280ft)	▲	3–4hr	Spring to autumn

Route No.	Route Title	Start/Finish	Distance
18	Javornik	Črni Vrh	21.5km (13¼ miles)
19	The Wine Region of Kras	Kobdilj	31.5km (19½ miles)
20	Komen and its surrounds	Komen	52km (32¼ miles)
21	Postojna classic	Postojna	31km (19¼ miles)
22	Lake Cerkno and the caves of Rakov Škocja	Dolenje Jezero	45.5km (28¼ miles)
23	Lake Cerknica circular	Dolenje Jezero	24km (15 miles)
24	Dolenjske Toplice and the Partisans' forest	Dolenjske Toplice	41.5km (25¾ miles)
25	Dolenjske Toplice and Soteska	Dolenjske Toplice	32km (19¾ miles)
Central and North East			
26	Velika Planina	Volovljek	18km (11 miles)
27	Menina Planina	Črnivec	38.5km (24 miles)
28	Jesenovo and Krvavica	Trojane	25.5km (15¾ miles)
29	The churches of Čreta	Nazarje	27km (16¾ miles)
30	The nature reserve of Pohorje	Matevžev Vrh	30km (18½ miles)
31	Maribor and its surroundings	Maribor old town square	26.5km (16½ miles)
32	The Maribor downhill park	Pohorje – bottom cable car station	15.5km (9½ miles)
33	The Najevnik Linden Tree	Črna na Koroškem	17.5km (11 miles)
34	The three valleys route	Črna na Koroškem	39.5km (24½ miles
35	Peca	Mitnik	16.5km (10¼ miles

% OFF ROAD	Ascent	Grade	Time	Time of Year
70	1035m (3395ft)	▲	1hr 30min–2hr 30min	Spring to autumn
60	705m (2315ft)	■	1hr 30min–2hr 30min	All year
70	1315m (4315ft)	▲	4–5hr	All year
40	575m (1885ft)	■	2hr 30min–3hr 30min	All year
80	1190m (3905ft)	▲	3–4hr 30min	Spring to autumn
55	380m (1245ft)	■	1–2hr	All year
75	1121m (3680ft)	▲	2hr 30min–3hr 30min	Spring to autumn
55	830m (2725ft)	■	2–3hr	Spring to autumn
100	780m (2560ft)	▲	2–2hr 30min	Late spring to early autumn
90	1340m (4395ft)	▲	3–4hr	Late spring to early autumn
40	1025m (3360ft)	■	1hr 30min–2hr 30min	All year
50	1370m (4495ft)	■	2hr 30min–3hr 30min	All year
100	680m (2230ft)	■	2–3hr	Spring to autumn
35	840m (2755ft)	■	2–2hr 30min	All year
90	950m (3115ft)	■/▲/◆	1–2hr	Late spring to early autumn
65	1045m (3430ft)	■	1–2hr	Spring to autumn
55	1925m (6315ft)	▲	4–5hr	Late spring to early autumn
90	835m (2740ft)	■	2–2hr 30min	Late spring to early autumn

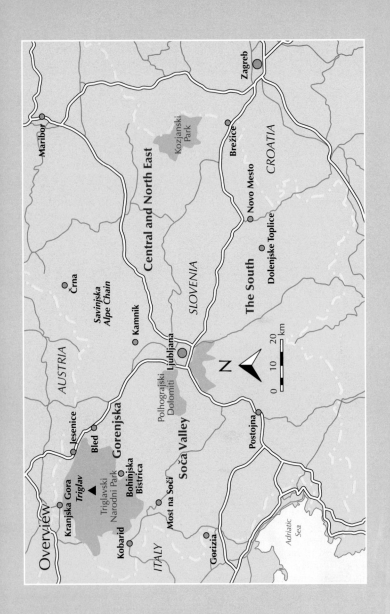

Introduction

Shhh! Don't tell anyone. I'm going to tell you a secret. There's a country slap in the middle of Europe that's beautiful, modern and well-developed, cheap to visit and that has some of the best mountain biking in the world. Oh, and it's beautiful – did I mention that? For some reason, however, most people planning their European holidays – especially those planning a biking trip abroad – mysteriously and unforgivably overlook Slovenia.

Those of you used to the beautifully groomed purpose-built trails of the UK, and maybe an annual trip to Spain or France for your yearly hit of rugged heights, may have certain questions to ask of a guide to Slovenian mountain biking. Not least of these might be, 'Why Slovenia?' and a supplementary query might be, 'Where is it?'. But this tiny country, nestled between Austria, Italy, Hungary and Croatia, has an enormous amount to offer the mountain biker.

At about the size of Wales, Slovenia is not big, yet as anyone who has ever visited either of these countries can attest, size doesn't always matter and small places can sometimes pack a surprising amount in. Within its compact area, for example, Slovenia can boast of three distinct climatic zones: Alpine (good for riding in), Mediterranean (good for relaxing days off and seafood) and Pannonian (good for wine and also for riding in). In amongst this, frankly, absurd abundance of climates can be found a huge variety of landscapes, from limestone karst to deep forest, from high mountains to meandering

Looking back at the Julian Alps from near the summit of Stol (Route 12)

On the Soča riverside trail (Route 10)

rivers. Did I mention that Slovenia was beautiful?

The Slovene people take all this nature very seriously. They are an outdoor nation and they punch well above their weight internationally in many sports, but especially in mountaineering, skiing and, of course, cycling. Conservation is also important to this country: around 50% of the land is covered in forest and much of the rest has been preserved to a very high degree. As a consequence, there is a great profusion of plant and wild life. To Britons, whose largest wild mammal is the red deer and whose most dangerous predator is the ferret, it may come as a bit of a shock to be riding a trail pocked with

the tracks of wolf, lynx, brown bear or chamois.

Slovenia also manages that strange balancing act of being very well developed while simultaneously remaining a cheap place to visit. It seceded from the former Yugoslavia in 1991, triggering the Balkan War. However, Slovenia itself only suffered 10 days of fighting and then emerged, miraculously fully formed, with a parliament, currency and national anthem later that year. It has remained a well-developed and relatively wealthy country ever since, joining the EU in 2004 and adopting the Euro.

Despite this, Slovenia is a cheap place for Britons to visit. There are budget airlines flying directly from the UK to the capital Ljubljana and to other airports in the region. A beer still only costs around €2, a pizza about €6 and a perfectly fine hardtail can be rented for something like €10 a day. Accommodation varies from luxury four- and five-star hotels and resorts to more modest but well-equipped campsites. In all cases, you'll be pleasantly surprised by the prices – especially if your experience of European travel is largely limited to the West.

But what of the riding? Well, of course, it's fabulous. The main regions all offer something different, catering for the competent beginner to the expert. The routes in this book reflect this diversity, although the majority are aimed at the fit and competent intermediate rider. Gorenjska provides possibly some of the most spectacular scenery in the country; it's all high mountains and lush valleys and you'll find that each day's ride begins with a stiff climb that can be up to 7 or 8km in length in places. The climbs tend to be done on gravel forestry tracks and they lead to fabulous views. Then, of course, you can benefit from all that climbing with an extended downhill run. It is classic alpine cross-country riding: nothing too technical but some tough physical challenges with awesome pay-offs.

The Soča Valley is a little bit different. The magnificent turquoise river defines this region and the tone of the rides change as you head further downstream. Higher up, where the river is a turbulent, troublesome teenager, you'll still get those long, high days out in the Alps with their tough climbs and long descents. As the river calms and begins to take its time, you'll find that the rides become a little less physically demanding

Flowers of the ancient woodland near Doljenske Toplice (Route 25)

The spectacular River Soča (Route 9)

from the southern edge all the way across to the Adriatic sea. Or you might be weaving your way in and out of vineyards in the warmth of a Mediterranean afternoon, looking forward to your seafood supper. There are the tremendous limestone caves of the Karst region around Postojna and the magical, ephemeral lake at Cerknica that disappears in the summer. None of these

(although no less rewarding). As you leave the national park, you'll also find a little more freedom in where you can ride and a few more single-track descents will creep in. Wherever I've been able, however, I have routed the trails alongside this most beautiful of rivers so that the rider can enjoy the full Soča experience.

Further south our routes flatten out somewhat and become a good deal more varied. You might find yourself riding among the forests of the Nanos plateau, where the undulating terrain belies the views you'll glimpse,

rides will overly tax your technical skills and, physically, they are generally much less demanding than the rides further north. This region is for relaxing days out and long, lazy evenings.

Finally we move to the central and north-east region, where the riding becomes a bit harder again. The Savinjske Alpe chain runs through this area and suddenly we're back on tough climbs and extended descents. The main difference with Gorenjska, however, is that these trails feel a good deal more remote as there are far fewer people around. The area around Črna, with its quiet alpine trails, may be the best the country has to offer but it is a bit out of the way. Maribor, however, cannot be said to be out of the way. There is a fantastic variety of riding to be had around the second city, from Nanos-esque plateau riding to the World Cup downhill course on the ski fields of Pohorje.

Purpose-built trails have grown in popularity in recent years and Slovenia has now become something of a haven for national mountain bike teams looking for quiet training grounds. However, many of the trails remain as adapted bridleways and retain an authentic, adventurous cross-country feel. You're as likely to find yourself tackling a 7km descent as you are to be following a turquoise river or winding through ancient forest. In addition, many of the ski resorts now provide summer downhill riding, using their uplift infrastructure to hoik your bike to the summit for you.

There's other great infrastructure for riders too. As well as the purpose-built trails there are good maps for all of the cycling regions, and the tourist information centres provide great advice. Bike hire or repair is also easy. Everywhere you go, there are well-stocked bike shops with knowledgeable staff (who almost certainly

speak English) and the gear and components you're used to.

In short, there really is no excuse for not going. Everything you could possibly require from a biking holiday is available in Slovenia. How about excellent and hearty food and drink? Got it. Fancy a ride in a cave? Sorted. What about a sauna after a day out on the hills? Check. Do you want all this and to pay less (a lot less) for it than you would in, say, France? Then stop faffing around, buy this guide and book your ticket.

GETTING THERE

Travelling with a bike
Travelling with a bike can be a hassle. If this is the first time you've taken

Almost empty trails await you: entering the village of Avber (Route 19)

an overseas mountain biking trip and you're thinking of taking your own bike, you should consider a few things. Firstly, you'll need to pack the bike well – particularly if you're flying. Many people simply buy or borrow a cardboard box from a bike shop and ship their machine in that. If you're planning to do that, make sure everything is well padded – particularly the rear mech and your lovely paintwork.

Another option is to buy a purpose-made bike box, which might set you back anything between £200 and £600. For that price,

Fancy a spot of cave biking? (Route 22)

however, they provide excellent protection for the bike while it's in transit. Do remember, if you're removing either of the wheels and you have hydraulic disc brakes, to put a spacer between the pads to prevent the calipers from locking shut.

It's also worth remembering that whatever means you've used to ship your bike out to Slovenia, you'll need to store the box somewhere until you're ready to bring the bike back in it. There is left-luggage at the major airports servicing Slovenia, but a car

at the other end might be the most practical solution.

Flying

Slovenia is well serviced by budget airlines, although the services change rapidly and new ones become available all of the time. At the time of writing, direct flights to the country's capital, Ljubljana, could be had from Stansted, Luton, Paris, Berlin, Vienna, Brussels, Copenhagen and many other cities in Europe. Flying from outside Europe, however, you'll need to head to one of the other regional hubs such as Venice, Trieste or Graz. The advantage of Slovenia is that, being small, it doesn't take long to get from one of these hubs to the trails. From Venice, it's about two hours by car to Slovenia; from Graz it's about one hour; and Trieste is virtually on the border.

Always check with your airline, before you book, how much it will cost to transport your bike. Prices and provision can vary and some of the budget airlines, in particular, can be a little tricky in the way the information is presented on their websites. You may choose to leave the bike at home, which shouldn't be a problem as all of the main trail areas have good bike-hire available.

Taking the train

If you're heading to Slovenia from one of the outer edges of Europe, catching the train is a relatively quick way of getting there without the hassle of airports and baggage limits. The simplest route from the UK is to take the Eurostar to Paris and from there to Strasbourg. From Strasbourg, there is an overnight train to Vienna and from there it's just a short trip to Jesenice in Slovenia and the heart of the mountains. The whole trip is less than two days. Other options from other parts of Europe are also possible but entry into the north at Jesenice or into Brežice from Zagreb are the easiest by far.

Always check the provision for bicycle carriage with the train companies before travelling as it can vary widely between countries – and even within them, depending on the type of service.

Driving

If you have the time, driving to Slovenia might be the best option if you have a lot to carry or you're heading there from a country not too far away.

The roads across most of Europe are excellent and Slovenia is well serviced with border entries along highways. You can enter from Italy at Gorizia or Trieste, from Austria at Villach, Wolfsberg or Graz, from Hungary into Lendava and from Croatia at a number of points. Of course, as Slovenia is in the Schengen zone, none of these crossings requires a passport. If cost or time is an issue, you can sleep in your vehicle at many of the motorway service stations along the way; this is commonly done on the continent and many of the stops have shower facilities.

GETTING AROUND

Assuming you haven't driven there, once you're in Slovenia it is perfectly possible to get about by public transport. However, it can be inconvenient for a mountain biker, particularly in rural areas. The buses don't always go exactly where you need them to and, in any case, can't carry a bike. The trains are good in Slovenia but there aren't many rail lines and they don't often go near the areas that we require, except for major towns such as Jesenice, Bled, Postojna or Maribor.

The best option, therefore, is probably to hire a car.

It's best to book a car before you leave home as great savings can be made by shopping around on online price comparison sites. Cars can be rented from all of the major cities in Slovenia (and some of the minor ones) as well as at airports and some train stations. If you're flying in to Italy or Austria and then planning to drive into Slovenia, do check in the rental terms and conditions that cross-border travel is allowed. Check also the cost of renting extra items such as bike racks, as this won't be included in the main agreement.

Information about trains within Slovenia can be found at www.slo-zeleznice.si/en and buses on the Slovenia tourist information site at www.slovenia.info/en. A good car rental comparison site is www.holidayautos.com.

WHEN TO GO

Slovenia is an extremely beautiful country at any time of the year but there are better times than others for mountain biking. The country is at its absolute best during spring and autumn (from the end of April until June and from September until the end of October). These also happen to be the cheapest times to visit. Summer will find many more services open, especially up in the mountains, but it can get pretty hot at times: 30 degrees is usual. Winter is likely to be too cold for all but the lowest rides. Even then, there is a good chance of standing snow in January and February.

Autumn can throw up some surprise conditions at this altitude (Route 8)

A friendly welcome at a traditional Slovenian hotel

ACCOMMODATION

Tourism is one of Slovenia's main industries and most of the rather functional hotels of the Socialist days are now gone or refurbished. As a consequence, there is a great deal of excellent accommodation available, from well-equipped campsites to five star hotels and everything in between. Again, price comparison sites are the best place to find deals on hotels, B&Bs and pensions (guest houses), but if you're looking for a hostel or a campsite, then the official tourist site, www.slovenia.info, has a lot of good information – including a section on accommodation specialising in cyclists (*kolesarski*). These specialist hotels and B&Bs are denoted by a system of cycle symbols: the more there

are, the better the facilities. Another option that many people are trying nowadays is Airbnb (www.airbnb. com), where local people rent out their spare rooms or holiday homes. Some great bargains are available.

These places are a good starting point for searching for accommodation, but there will also be some of my own personal recommendations in each of the region sections. For additional information, see Appendix B.

FOOD AND DRINK

If you have any concerns about the quality of the food in a former Socialist country, then please don't. You'll find a selection of excellent restaurants in most towns. There won't be a wide variety of cuisines available (for example, outside of Ljubljana, you're unlikely to find a curry) – a quirk of the relative lack of racial diversity in the country. However, you will find Italian, Hungarian and Serbian dishes, and the local cuisine tends to be hearty (if not always healthy) alpine food. There are usually good vegetarian options too.

Lunch is usually the main meal of the day for Slovenes, and a great option for a filling meal is *kosilo*. Often offered at restaurants and hotels, kosilo is a set menu with a soup to start, a help-yourself salad bar and a filling main course. They represent great value.

The water from the taps in Slovenia is good to drink and there is also an excellent locally-based mineral water company, Radenska. The mountains are predominantly limestone, so it is sometimes difficult to find water en route. It can be expensive to buy bottled water in the mountains, so do fill up before heading off.

New twists on old classics in Slovenian cuisine

Of course, after the ride, there is also great beer and wine. For beer (*pivo*), the locals mostly drink either Laško or Union; however, many microbreweries have sprung up in recent years offering excellent alternatives. Wine (*vino*) has been a part of Slovenian culture since the Roman times and they make excellent demi-sec whites and fresh, interesting reds.

LANGUAGE

The language of Slovenia is, not surprisingly, Slovene. It's a very close relative of Serbo-Croat, the old language of Yugoslavia, and English-speaking visitors are unlikely to find anything familiar in it. Not to fear, however; not only is there a handy glossary at the back of this book (see Appendix A) but, in almost all parts of Slovenia, English is spoken very well by the locals. You really shouldn't have a problem, but you may feel that a pocket guide to the language would be a useful addition to your luggage.

MONEY

Since joining the European Union in 2004, Slovenia has used the Euro as its currency. There are several banks in Slovenia, most of which have a branch in the major towns. Smaller towns are likely only to have a branch of the local bank, but there will be an ATM so you're pretty much guaranteed to be able to get money out in all but the smallest of towns. Alternatively, most places, including many of the mountain huts, will accept card payments.

A brief water break by the River Nadiža (Route 10)

Slovenia is cheap, especially outside of the tourist traps of Bled and Ljubljana. Expect to pay around €2 for a beer; a coffee (served as an espresso unless you stipulate otherwise) will be about €1.50; a pizza is around €6; a kosilo will be around about €10–15, as will a main course at dinner time. Of course, you can pay more than this at smart restaurants and hotels, but there shouldn't be any need. Bike parts may be a touch more expensive relative to food. Generally, an inner tube will cost around €3–6 and a bottle of lube around €7; in other words, about the same as much of Europe.

EQUIPMENT

If you're planning a mountain bike holiday abroad, you're probably already pretty au fait with the gear that you need for a day's riding. However, as a recap and a potential aide memoire for those who might be riding in the high mountains for the first time, here are some recommendations on kit.

Bike

Bike hire in Slovenia is pretty easy and relatively cheap. There are a number of options for hire, and some suggestions will be made at the beginning of each region section.

Always perform a pre-ride bike check. This is especially important when travelling overseas as you have either transported your bike (and thus dismantled and reassembled it) or you've hired a bike with which you might not be familiar. If you're not sure how to go about a pre-ride check, it's worth looking up

A hardtail suitable for the Slovenian trails

the 'M-Check' on the internet. This is a thorough going-over that you give your bike which traces a rough 'M' shape around the bike and will help you to remember all the parts you need to review.

Clothing

If you're a regular road-rider, you might think that the most important decision about clothing is the colour scheme. Mountain bikers tend to be a bit more pragmatic, and practicality has to play a greater part in decision-making.

I would suggest the following are essential pieces of clothing:

- helmet – well fitted and less than five years old. If there is any visible wear it should be discarded, and if the helmet has been involved in an accident, even if there is no visible damage, it should be replaced.
- gloves – to prevent injury in the event of a fall and to protect from the cold if necessary.
- shoes – sturdy outdoor shoes at least, but ideally specialist shoes with an inflexible sole.
- glasses – to protect the eyes from sunlight as well as mud and stones; a pair with interchangeable lenses for different light conditions is ideal.
- padded shorts – either close-fitting or baggy to provide comfort for your day in the saddle.

In addition, comfortable, quick-drying clothes will make your ride more pleasant and it is always worth packing a spare warm layer for the mountaintops and a lightweight waterproof for the occasional shower.

Some people – especially those who are into downhill – would also consider wearing body armour. I would say it wasn't essential kit unless you're intending to ride specific downhill routes that tend to be very technical and come with a high chance of falling off.

Everything else

Riding a mountain bike can take you to fairly remote spots, so self-sufficiency is important. A tool kit is vital to get you out of common mechanical problems and as a minimum it should include:

- a couple of spare inner tubes
- tyre-levers
- a pump
- a compact bike tool with a range of Allen keys
- a chain tool and spare link

Mountain biking can be dangerous. Carrying a first aid kit is not only a sensible precaution, but I would count it as essential. It needn't be large but it should contain the following:

- sterile wipes for wound cleaning
- plasters/band-aids
- larger wound dressings (self-adhesive)
- triangular bandage (for slings and limb immobilisation)
- antiseptic
- paracetamol (or other painkiller)
- rehydration sachets
- fully charged mobile phone (local emergency number 112)

Trailside repairs aren't so bad under these conditions (Route 10)

- EHIC (European Health Insurance Card), which allows access to local health services for free

Of course, it's also important to know what to do with these items so, if you don't already know, book yourself onto a first aid course.

Finally, food and drink are, obviously, essential additions to your backpack. You may have to carry your lunch with you if the route doesn't take you past any hostelries but, in any case, you should always carry a few high-energy snacks with you as well as plenty of water. In the Alps of Slovenia, where it can be both hot and frustratingly free of streams, at least two litres would be a sensible precaution.

WAYMARKING

Many of the rides in this book make mention of waymarked routes and cycle route signs. While there is a wealth of marked routes, these signs cannot be relied on in general. The local municipalities are responsible for creating, maintaining and signing cycle routes; many of the municipalities are very good at this but, frustratingly, there is no national system for signage. So in Kobarid you might be following a blue circle with a white bike in it, and in Vipava you might be following a stylised orange cyclist. If you check in at the local tourist information centres they will be able to give you a good idea of how extensive the network of marked routes is in that area.

Signage varies depending on the municipality

Maps

The maps in this book have all been provided by Kartografija and are extracts of their series of 1:75,000 scale maps reproduced at a scale of 1:50,000 for ease of use. When a map is referenced at the beginning of each route, it is the Kartografija 1:75,000 that is being named. These are the maps I would recommend that you carry, and there are only eight of them to cover the entire country. However, there are also 1:50,000 and 1:25,000 scale maps available from both Kartografija and from Geodetski Zavod Slovenije (the national geological survey). All of these can be bought from Amazon or a specialist map shop such as Stanfords (www.stanfords.co.uk).

In addition, you might want to go paper-free and use your smartphone for additional navigational help. There are a number of apps available for this purpose but, in most cases, you will have to buy the map of Slovenia from the service provider. One example is ViewRanger GPS (iOS and android); the app shows you in real time (on very clear maps) where you are and you can create routes. The whole of Slovenia can be bought at 1:50,000 for US$42.99.

EMERGENCY SITUATIONS

Should the worst happen, it is vital you know what to do. All across Europe, the emergency services number is 112, and from this you can access the fire service, ambulances and emergency vets. The police are on 113 and mountain rescue on 140. In all cases, the calls can be held in English. For all likely bike-related incidents, this should cover you but it is also worth noting that should you have a car accident, as a foreigner, you will need to call the police. If it's not an emergency, the contact details of medical centres can be found in Appendix C; there will always be English speakers in those centres.

It makes sense to get travel insurance for any trip to Slovenia. While there is reciprocal health care through the European Health Insurance Card or EHIC (for the time being at least – Brexit may alter this), it is always a good idea to take out extra insurance. This could also include third party liability and protection for your bike if you're taking it.

USING THIS GUIDE

Each region described in this guide has its own distinctive feel, as we'll see shortly. However, this guide is designed for riders with a general interest in mountain biking. There aren't many rides for the absolute beginner in here, but then there aren't many rides for the hardcore extremist either. Most of the routes included fall into the cross-country style of riding and, while they often require a decent level of fitness, they generally aren't too technical.

The regions

This guide has been split into four regions to cluster rides together. These regions are a touch artificial but they do give an idea of which rides are accessible from where. Slovenia is a small country; you could drive right across it in less than a day. However, to make journeys shorter, you may wish to base yourself in one region and do the rides within it. Alternatively, if you happen to be on holiday in Slovenia and you fancy a day out riding, these regions give you a rough idea of what's accessible from wherever you're staying.

The routes

Each ride is written as a self-contained, circular route with a place to park at the start and returning to the car at the end. All the salient information about the route, such as distance, height gained and grade, is presented at the beginning in its own box. There is also a profile to give you an idea of the route's hills and descents, but please note that the scales on each profile are not necessarily the same as any of the other rides. Finally, there is the route description itself: pertinent directions presented in paragraphs that break the ride up into manageable chunks.

The grading

Each ride is given a grade similar to those used at British trail centres. Blue is easiest, followed by red and then black.

In Britain, however, the grade is largely to tell you only how technical the route is. In Slovenia, many of the routes are not especially technical but may become quite remote or require a high degree of physical fitness. The grades used in this book, therefore, can be summarised as follows:

■ technically not difficult and the route is not remote. Only a reasonable amount of fitness is required to complete this ride.

▲ this route might have technical elements to it. It might require a higher level of fitness or it might take in more remote locations. There may be highly technical sections but they will be short and can be walked around.

◆ this ride should only be tackled by people confident in their riding skills and their fitness. It is likely to be remote and to require a high level of fitness. There may, in addition, be highly technical sections.

ABBREVIATIONS AND SYMBOLS USED IN THE ROUTE DESCRIPTIONS

← left
→ right
↑ straight ahead
• Mentions of left and right (and left-hand and right-hand), other than specific directions, are given thus: 'where the road curves to the **right** ignore the turning on your left-hand side, instead go ↑ onto a farm track'.

• Easy-to-miss paths are noted in **bold green**; warnings of steep, dangerous or possibly crowded routes in **bold red**.
• Place names in route descriptions that appear on their maps are noted in **bold**.
• Important signs along the way are noted in *red italics* in route descriptions.

Enjoying the easy descent on the way back to the start of Route 6

Gorenjska

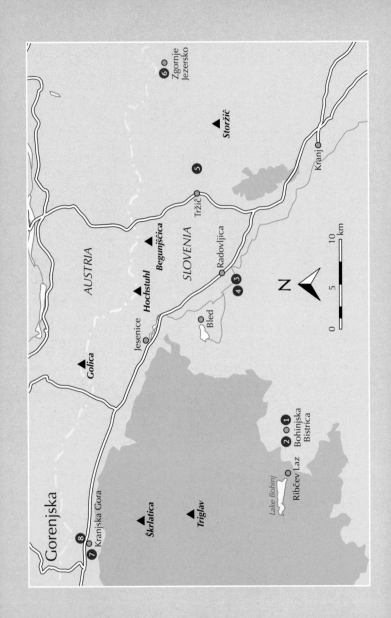

The high alpine meadow at Uskavnica (Route 1)

If you were only allowed to visit one part of Slovenia, it would probably be Gorenjska. If you have already visited Slovenia, it was probably Gorenjska. The region is up in the mountains and contains some of the most spectacular scenery anywhere in Slovenia. From the fairytale Lake Bled to the mighty Sava River to the ski resort of Kranjska Gora, everywhere you look there's something to arrest the eye. Apart from Ljubljana, Gorenjska is the most popular destination for tourists to the country; however, unless you're in Bled on a Saturday in the middle of the season, you're unlikely to feel crowded out. Relatively speaking, this is still an unknown gem.

Kranj (pronounced Kran) is the largest city in the region but it still isn't huge. It has some good options for places to stay and it's right next to the international airport and the motorway system. It is not, however, very inspiring and you'd be much better off staying in Bled. This town is much more central for the rides in this guide and it is spectacular, clinging to the shore of a thermal lake in the middle of which sits an old monastery on an island. Rising sheer from the shores of the lake is a cliff atop which rests a castle. If that's not enough to convince you, it's also home of the famous cake *kremna rezina* (we'd know it as a vanilla slice).

ACCOMMODATION

As the main tourist location in the region, Bled has plenty of options for accommodation. The town has a range of hotels, many of which are owned by the same chain. The best of these is the Grand Hotel Toplice, but if your budget doesn't quite run to five star, a better option would be Hotel Jelovica, a budget hotel with great lake views and a central location. Around the other side of the lake is Camping Bled, a campsite with very good facilities and a party atmosphere in season.

Further up the Sava valley you'll find the bigger, more secluded Lake Bohinj. If you don't mind being a little bit out of the way, there's a budget hotel and hostel on the shores of the lake called Hostel Pod Voglem, which has a friendly service and bike wash facilities.

Finally, you may want to base yourself in Kranjska Gora right up in the north-west corner where Slovenia meets Italy and Austria. There are plenty of hotel options in the town, including the excellent Hotel Lek. For those on a tighter budget, however, Hostel Barovc is just a short walk out of town and has most things you'd need.

Services

There is a tourist information centre in all of the bigger towns in the area, including Bled, Bohinj, Jesenice, Kranj and Kranjska Gora. They provide excellent information and are a good source for maps as well as very good publications on other tourist attractions.

Most towns in the region will have somewhere to hire bikes, but the best place is, without a doubt, 3glav (pronounced tree-glau) Adventures (www.3glav-adventures.com). Based in Bled, they have the best hire bikes that I've come across in the region and they are also a rich source of information about biking and other activities in the area.

Alternatively, you could try Bike Park Kranjska Gora (www.bike-park.si), the base of operations for the downhill courses in the town. They are also able to help with accommodation.

Emergencies

There are good health centres and clinics as well as pharmacies in all of the following towns: Bled, Bohinj, Jesenice, Kranj, Kranjska Gora and Radovljica. Further information can be found at www.slovenian-alps.com/en/info/health-care.

Route 1
The high alpine at Uskovnica

START/FINISH	Mercator supermarket, Bohinjska Bistrica
DISTANCE	33.75km (21 miles)
ON ROAD	8.75km (5½ miles)
OFF ROAD	25km (15½ miles)
ASCENT	1380m (4530ft)
GRADE	▲
TIME	3–4hr
MAP	Alpski Svet – Zahodni Del
REFRESHMENTS	Planina koča na Uskovnici (in season) or Bohinjska Bistrica
PARKING	At the supermarket

OVERVIEW

This route is one of the most spectacular in the whole book. It begins easily enough by taking the new cycle path out of Bohinjska Bistrica through the attractive Sava valley towards Ribčev Laz and Lake Bohinj. There is, however, a tough 8.5km climb following that warm-up. This climb brings you up into the high alpine pastures, where you're treated to spectacular vistas of the surrounding mountains and the picturesque cowherd villages of Uskovnica and Zajamniki, and then a single-track descent back to the road at Podjelje. Do not forget your camera.

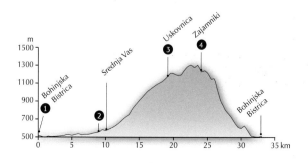

Directions

1 Leave the supermarket car park and turn ←
onto the main road through town. Just after the
bridge, look out for the sign saying *Kolarški Pot*
(just before the excellent Kamp Danica) and
turn →. After crossing another, wooden bridge,
turn ← and follow the blue cycle signs towards
Srednja Vas, roughly following the Ribnica
upstream.

2 After about 9km you'll reach a main road. Go
↑, crossing the main road onto the smaller
one opposite, and at the next T-junction turn
→ through **Studor**, again following the blue
signs. At the next T-junction, turn ← and then
← again at the *Ribnica* sign. This brings you
onto the bottom of the climb. Follow first the
road and then the track all the way to the tiny
chapel and water trough about 8.5km later at
the mountain hut at **Uskovnica**. Rest and refill
your water bottle here before heading towards
Zajamniki.

Thankful to crest the rise after the 8.5km climb

Slap Mostnice

Izvir Krope

Pl. koča na Vojah
690

Korita Mostnice

Hudičev most

Ledeniške
morene

Planšarski
muzej

STARA FUŽINA

JEZERO

Sv. Janez Krstnik

RIBČEV LAZ

V. Grad
684

Pl. v Strženih

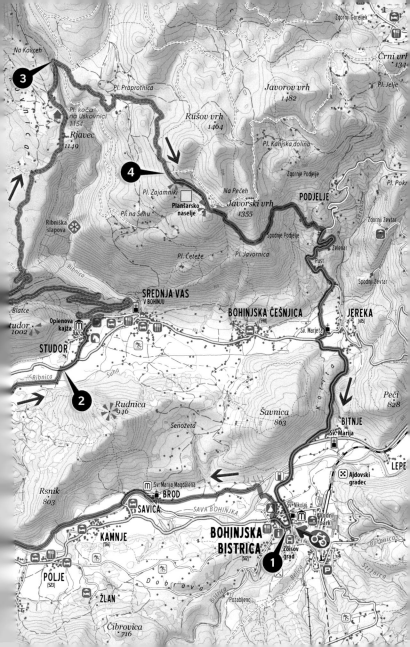

3 Take the trail leading off to the → until you come to a fork and then take the → downhill. At the next fork, take the ←. When you arrive at the next T-junction turn →, following the sign for *Zajamniki*. After about 3km, turn → at the sign for *Prva Pomoč* and this will bring you into the village of **Zajamniki**. Make a little time here to take in the spectacular views and the quaint village.

On the descent from Zajamniki

4 At the end of the village, turn ← and then take the → fork. After around 500 metres, at the painted rock, turn → and then enjoy the 4km or so of singletrack descent. At the next T-junction, turn → and follow this to the main road at the bottom of the descent. At the road, next to the church of **Sv Marjeta**, turn → and then immediately ←. At the next T-junction at **Bitnje**, turn → and follow the road back to the car park at **Bohinjska Bistrica**.

Route 2
In the foothills of Črna Prst

START/FINISH	Mercator supermarket, Bohinjska Bistrica
DISTANCE	26.5km (16½ miles)
ON ROAD	6.5km (4¼ miles)
OFF ROAD	20km (12¼ miles)
ASCENT	1130m (3705ft)
GRADE	▲
TIME	2–3hr
MAP	Alpski Svet – Zahodni Del
REFRESHMENTS	Bohinjska Bistrica (bring a packed lunch)
PARKING	At the supermarket

75%
OFF ROAD

OVERVIEW

This route will take you to the quieter side of the Sava valley. Leaving from the popular tourist town of Bohinjska Bistrica, it heads out past the ski resort of Kobla and up onto the forested foothills of the impressive mountain Črna Prst (meaning 'black soil'). Having made the tough climb, you're rewarded with views down the valley and to the mountains on the other side – and, of course, with a long descent. Once back down into the valley, you return to the start via pretty meadows typical of the Sava region.

DIRECTIONS

1 Out of the supermarket car park turn →, taking the road that leads past Tuš and the Aquapark. Follow this road until you turn → just before it crosses the

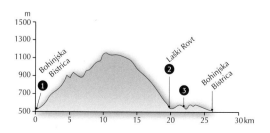

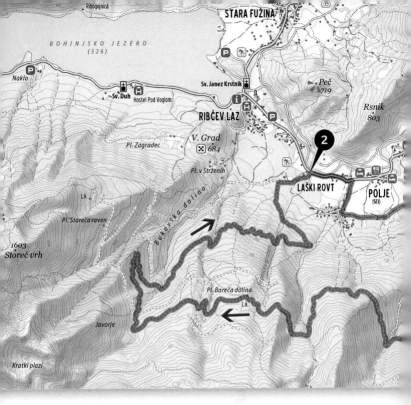

railway, following the sign for *Kobla* ski area. Your climb starts here, firstly for 2km on the road and then, once you've passed the car park for **Kobla**, for another 8km off-road except for a few false flats. Follow the forest track until you begin a gentle descent off the plateau of **Bareča Dolina**. About 10km after the ski resort, take the ➔ fork and start the **steep descent** back to the valley, turning ➔ at the next T-junction.

② Once you reach the main road at **Laški Rovt**, turn ➔ and then first ➔ past the Gostišče Pr' Kosnik. Take the ⬅ fork into the little settlement (actually the far edge of Laški Rovt) and then look out for the sign for *20 Bohinjska Bistrica* on the ⬅. Follow this road straight until it becomes a track (don't follow the road round to the left). Continue straight, skirting the woods where possible, until the next T-junction where you turn ➔, following the sign *20 Žlan, Bohinjska Bistrica*.

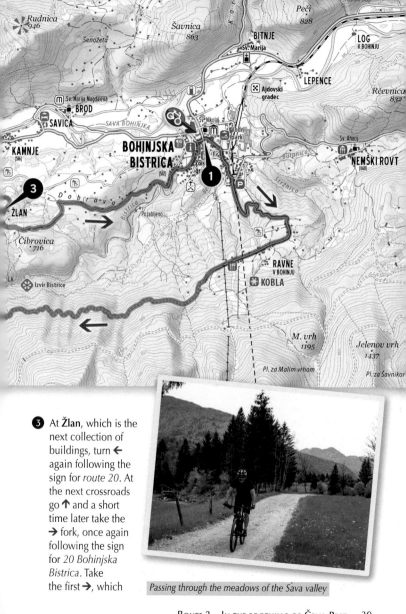

3 At **Žlan**, which is the next collection of buildings, turn ← again following the sign for *route 20*. At the next crossroads go ↑ and a short time later take the → fork, once again following the sign for *20 Bohinjska Bistrica*. Take the first →, which

Passing through the meadows of the Sava valley

Slogging up the ascent

comes just after a pretty farm, and then, a little further on, turn ← onto the road. Follow this road through the village, keeping the small river (the Bistrica) on your right until you meet the main road. Turn → and follow this back to the car park in **Bohinjska Bistrica**.

Route 3
Across the Jelovica Plateau

<table>
<tr><td>**Start/Finish**</td><td>Sveti Trojica (church), Kamna Gorica</td></tr>
<tr><td>**Distance**</td><td>38km (23½ miles)</td></tr>
<tr><td>**On road**</td><td>12km (7½ miles)</td></tr>
<tr><td>**Off road**</td><td>26km (16 miles)</td></tr>
<tr><td>**Ascent**</td><td>1570m (5150ft)</td></tr>
<tr><td>**Grade**</td><td>▲</td></tr>
<tr><td>**Time**</td><td>3–4hr</td></tr>
<tr><td>**Map**</td><td>Alpski Svet – Zahodni Del</td></tr>
<tr><td>**Refreshments**</td><td>Goška Ravan (in season) or Vodiška Planina (all year)</td></tr>
<tr><td>**Parking**</td><td>Car park on main road from Radovljica, just before Kamna Gorica</td></tr>
</table>

Overview

During World War II, Jelovica was a favourite hiding place for the Partisans as they fought their guerrilla war against the Nazis. Following this route, you'll see why as you head up onto the wild plateau. Again, it's a tough climb but the top yields a network of trails leading through the forest. Lunch is possible at one of the best spots in the mountains: the Partisan-built refuge at Vodiška Planina. Returning to the road via a tricky descent, you're treated to great views of the church on the hill, Sveti Primož. From there, it's back through the industrial revolution towns of Kropa and Kamna Gorica to your car.

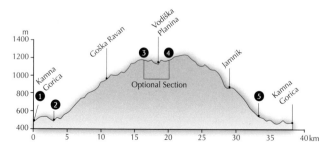

DIRECTIONS

1 From the car park at the church of Sv Trojica turn →, and after 100m turn ← at the sign for *111 Radovljica*. At the crossroads, go ↑ then → into the woods and up the hill and → again at the road. Follow this road until it runs out at a farm and take the track on the **RH** side of the buildings (this is the very end of the village of **Na Dobravi**). Following the *Kolesarska Pot* signs, turn → then ← and, at the fork, take the ← again. Just after this, the track becomes road again and you follow this down to the main road where you turn ← and then first → following the sign for *Route 103*.

2 Follow the road through the village of Spodnja until you cross the river for the second time. Just after this, the road becomes a trail again and you begin your 7km climb. About 3km later, at the fork, turn ← following the sign for *Goški Ravni*. After a further 3km you'll come to another fork; turn ← and continue climbing towards Goška Ravan. **Goška Ravan** itself arrives a short time later with the welcome sight of a mountain inn: feel free to take refreshments here before carrying on. At the next two junctions keep to the →, following the *Kolesarska Pot* signs until finally arriving at a junction with a sign for *Vodice* around 5.5km from Goška Ravan.

This mountain inn is a welcome sight on reaching Goška Ravan

Descending to the road at Jamnik

3 From here it is possible to continue straight on and shorten your ride by 4km, but I would recommend visiting the Partisan refuge (and restaurant) at Vodiška Planina by turning ← here. Follow this trail until you reach the **inn**, which is open all year. Follow the trail back to the same junction.

4 Turn ← once you get back to the junction. At the crossroads, turn ← and then → after the *Pot* signs and then ← at the next T-junction. **Watch out: although most of this ride is blue, this section is a tricky descent at red grade.** At the following T-junction, turn ← again and follow this down to the main road just above the village of **Jamnik** where you turn ←.

5 After around 3km, having descended the steep section on the road and just as you enter the town of **Kropa**, take the steep ramp up to the left past the church. Follow this road until it becomes bike route 105 and follow this until you get to a T-junction near to **Brezovica** and turn ←. Turn ← again and then follow this main road back to **Kamna Gorica**. On the outskirts of town, it is possible to continue on the main road to the car park, but I would recommend turning ←, following the bike route sign, into town to admire the watermill. Follow the road through town back to the car park.

Route 4
To the Crone's Tooth

START/FINISH	Sveti Trojica (church), Kamna Gorica
DISTANCE	35.5km (22 miles)
ON ROAD	4.5km (2¾ miles)
OFF ROAD	31km (19¼ miles)
ASCENT	1315m (4315ft)
GRADE	◆
TIME	3–4hr
MAP	Alpski Svet – Zahodni Del
REFRESHMENTS	Vodiška Planina (all year)
PARKING	Car park on right-hand side of main road from Radovljica, just before Kamna Gorica

OVERVIEW

Beginning and ending at the same point as the last route, this trip covers some of the same ground but includes a fabulous view out over Lake Bled to the mountains beyond once you've reached Babji Zob (the Crone's Tooth). After the climbing and exploring, treat yourself to a hearty lunch and maybe a glass of something at the Partisan-built refuge at Vodiška Planina. The vast majority of this ride is blue grade at most, but be warned: the descent from the Vodiška Planina is most definitely a red and the remoteness pushes the grade overall up to black.

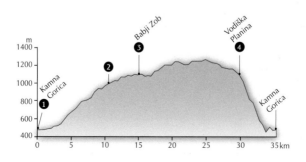

Directions

1 From the car park at the church of Sv Trojica, turn ← back onto the main road towards Radovljica. Take the second ←, signposted for cycle route *103 Talež and Vodice*, and follow this road through the village of Spodnja until it becomes a gravel track. This is the beginning of your climb. After climbing for around 3km, turn ← at the first fork, following the sign for *Planinski Dom* (you can take a diversion here to Talež, about 800m away, for good food and a great view). Continue climbing to the next fork where you turn →, following the sign for *Ribinska Planina*.

2 The worst of the climbing is behind you now. Follow the track to an alpine hut in the crux of a fork and turn →. After another couple of kilometres turn ← at the next fork, following the sign for *Babji Zob*, and follow the same sign at the next fork, turning →. Take the next major → and follow this to a fork with a large rock with 'Ricman' written on it; turn → and follow the trail through the top of the meadow. The trail eventually becomes singletrack and, ultimately, you need to walk the last couple of hundred metres but the view from here over Lake Bled is well worth the effort. This is **Babji Zob**. Just off the steep footpath that leads back down towards Bled below you is an extensive limestone cave system. If you have the time (and the legs) to visit, it is worth a look.

The alpine meadow Ricman

3 Return the way you came, back to the main track off which you turned right. Turn →. Through the next set of forks, all coming in around 2km, you need to turn ← (following the sign for *Bohinj*), then → and then ← again, this time following the sign *Razen za koleskarje*. At the

The bikes take a rest at Babji Zob

next T-junction turn ← and head downhill before turning ← again at the next T-junction about 1km further on. After around another 5km turn → at the fork, following the sign for *Planinska Dom*, and take the track beneath the slopes of **Dovski Vrh**. Turn ← downhill at the next fork and then, at the staggered junction, go ↑, following the sign for *Vodice*. Follow this trail all the way to the mountain inn called **Partizanski Dom**. Take a well-earned break and try the *jota* (bean and sauerkraut stew).

4 Having refreshed yourself, head ← downhill (**be warned, most of this section is singletrack and it is used by walkers**). After only about 300m there is a three-way fork and you want to continue ↑. A short way after this, at the next fork, turn ←, following the sign for *Kamna Gorica*. After about 1km take the **easy-to-miss** trail downhill on the →. This will bring you to a hairpin track; on the apex of the second hairpin take the **easy-to-miss** →, following the red-and-white roundels on the trees. This trail will bring you out to a road at **Miklavževec** just to the north of Brezovica; turn ← and then ← again at the main road. Follow this main road all the way back to the car park at **Kamna Gorica**.

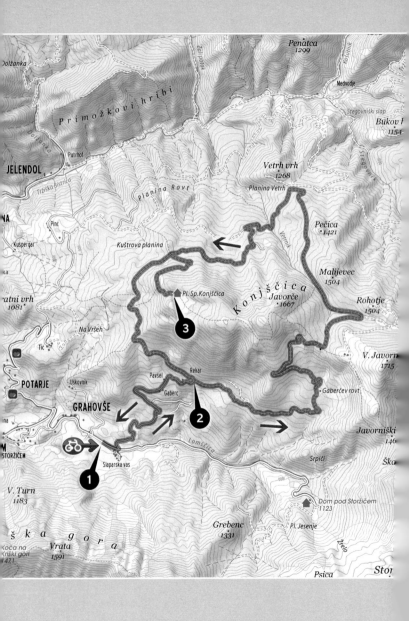

Route 5
Grahovše circular

START/FINISH	Parking area near Grahovše
DISTANCE	21.75km (13½ miles)
ON ROAD	0.75km (½ mile)
OFF ROAD	21km (13 miles)
ASCENT	1355m (3725ft)
GRADE	■
TIME	2–2hr 30min
MAP	Alpski Svet – Zahodni Del
REFRESHMENTS	Planina Sp. Konjščica (in season)
PARKING	Off-road parking on left-hand side of road between Grahovše and Slaparska Vas

OVERVIEW

Over on the quieter side of the Slovenian Alps, this ride is a quick but tough blast through the forests and up to the high alpine pastures. This region is known for its cheese, and the highlight of this route is the small mountain *gostilna*, or inn, at Planina Konjščica, where you can try the hearty local food.

DIRECTIONS

1 From the parking area turn ← onto the road. The road quickly becomes a track, after which take the first ←, signposted for *Turistična Kmetija Rekar*. The climbing begins immediately and goes on for about 3km. Your first brief respite comes just after a toll barrier (which cyclists can go around) at the T-junction. Turn → here (signposted for *Planina Javornik*) and enjoy the easier angle of slope for a while.

Still a long way to climb!

② Follow the forest trail as you begin to climb again, passing through **Gaberčevrovt**, and go through the gate about 4km from the last junction. Roughly another 1km further on, turn ⬅ at a T-junction near to **Rohotje** and

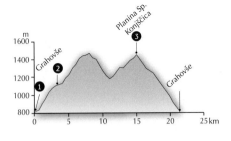

begin a descent. At the bottom of the descent, at **Planina Vetrh**, turn ⬅ at the T-junction (to the right there is parking). After about another kilometre, turn ⬅ back on yourself, following the sign for *Planina Konjščica*. Take the ⬅ (again signposted for *Planina Konjščica*) and follow the track to the dead end at the alpine meadow. Treat yourself to lunch at **Planina Konjščica**.

③ Return the way you came back to the main track and turn ⬅. This will take you, about 2km later, to the junction near to the toll barrier. Turn ➡ and follow the route by which you ascended, all the way back to your point of departure near **Grahovše**.

A welcome sight at the planina

Route 6
Lake Zgornje

START/FINISH	Memorial car park, Zgornje Jezersko
DISTANCE	13.5km (8½ miles)
ON ROAD	4km (2½ miles)
OFF ROAD	9.5km (6 miles)
ASCENT	380m (1245ft)
GRADE	■
TIME	30min–1hr
MAP	Alpski Svet – Zahodni Del
REFRESHMENTS	Planšarsko Jezero (all year)
PARKING	Opposite memorial on right-hand side of road approaching Zgornje Jezersko from Kranj

70%
OFF ROAD

OVERVIEW

A gentle jaunt in the mountains, this route eases its way along a valley and up a small hill. Meanwhile, you're surrounded by spectacular mountains and your journey takes in a beautiful lake. While it won't test your technical abilities, this ride will pass a very pleasant hour and will also allow you the opportunity to eat at the fabulous lakeside restaurant at Planšarsko Jezero.

DIRECTIONS

1 Head away from the main road, down the small hill to the **right** of the car park (as seen from the road). Turn ← straight after the little bridge and then, at the T-junction with the road, turn →. Follow this road and trail until you reach the car park for the restaurant at **Planšarsko Jezero**. In the car park, turn ← and cross the little bridge and then immediately turn →.

2 As this road bears away from the lake, take the → onto the gravel track and look out for the **easy-to-miss** → about 100m later. Cross the wooden bridge (making

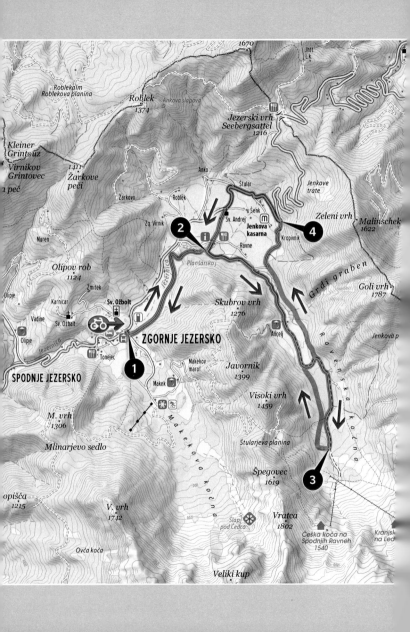

A gentle route in the high mountains

sure you check out the view back to the lake as you cross) and bear ← to the road and then turn ←. This road becomes a gravel track; after you've passed the tourist farm **Ancelj** and about 2km of steady climbing, follow it as it bears 90 degrees to the ← (going straight on is the descent route) and then follow it round to the →, following signs for the parking. At the next fork, follow the signs for *Parkirišče Češka Koča* to the →. This will take you to the car park at the beginning of the many walking routes.

3 Pass straight through the car park and take the next →, signposted *Sprehojalna Pot,* and then turn immediately →. This is the beginning of the descent; enjoy the 2km of this easy flowing run. Turn ← at the only junction (past a big boulder on the **right**) and you'll all too quickly come back out onto the gravel road that you ascended on. Turn → and then, as

Heading home

the track bends to the **right**, turn ← through the fence. Again, enjoy the gentle pleasure of this next easy descent through woods and open meadows towards the village of Kropivnik.

4 At the T-junction with the road, turn →, following signs for *Kmetiji Jenk, Jenkova Kasarna – muzej*. Follow the same signs at the next junction and turn ←. Pass through the tiny village of **Kropivnik** and then, at the T-junction with the main road, turn ←. Follow the main road as far as the church (**St Andrej**) and turn ← just in front of it. Follow this to the car park at **Planšarsko Jezero** and make a stop for your refreshments with a view (I recommend the *štruklji* – filled rolls). After your break, follow the trail you originally came in on back to the car in **Zgornje Jezersko**.

Route 7
Peč and the three borders

START/FINISH	Bike Park, Kranjska Gora
DISTANCE	25.5km (15¾ miles)
ON ROAD	10km (6¼ miles)
OFF ROAD	15.5km (9½ miles)
ASCENT	1050m (3445ft)
GRADE	■
TIME	2–3hr
MAP	Alpski Svet – Zahodni Del
REFRESHMENTS	Peč (May to September)
PARKING	Bike Park car park, on the edge of Kranjska Gora

OVERVIEW

The top left-hand corner of Slovenia meets both Austria and Italy at one point: Mt Peč (which means oven). It's a popular hiking spot and in the winter it has skiing. Because of that, there are ski lifts (from the Austrian side) and the associated bars. There are also some spectacular views out over the three countries. It's quite a climb to get up there (though not technical) but well worth the effort.

DIRECTIONS

1 From the car park, head away from town on the bike route that runs at the bottom of the ski runs. Turn ➜ for Podkoren next to the piste map noticeboard. At the crossroads with the main road go ⬆, and at the next

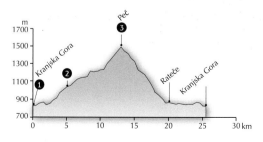

crossroads, next to Hotel Vitranc in **Podkoren**, go ↑ again. Follow this road until it meets the main road and turn ← up the hill. About 1.5km further on, turn ← off the road onto a gravel track just before the 1km roadside marker.

2 Follow this track first down and then up through the woods. After about 5km turn →, back on yourself, at the sign for *Tromeja* (facing the other way). This is the beginning of the tough climb up to the summit. At a saddle near the peak you'll see the refreshment huts on the right-hand side. Continue to the top of **Peč** where you'll find the commemoration of the three borders. Enjoy the view, then make your way back to the huts for lunch.

A commemoration of the three borders

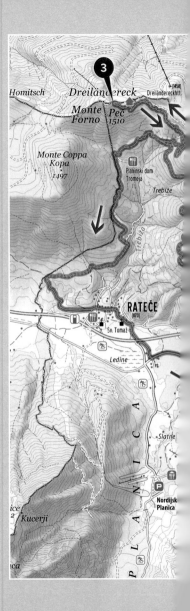

The spectacular Julian Alps

❸ Return back down the track (looking out for the fabulous views of the Julian Alps) and, at the bottom where you joined it (at the sign for *Tromeja*), turn →. Follow the bicycle route 8 signs all the way to the bottom of the hill at **Rateče** (more lunch options here) and, at the T-junction, turn ←. Follow the bicycle route D-2 signs through the village and, at the main road, continue ↑ onto the cycle and pedestrian path. At the next crossroads, turn ← (again following the D-2 sign) and ride this route all the way back to the car park at **Kranjska Gora**.

Route 8
Kranjska Gora circular

START/FINISH	Sporty Bar, Kranjska Gora
DISTANCE	27km (16¾ miles)
ON ROAD	9km (5½ miles)
OFF ROAD	18km (11¼ miles) – including paved cycle-paths
ASCENT	1405m (4610ft)
GRADE	▲
TIME	1hr 30min–2hr 30min
MAP	Alpski Svet – Zahodni Del
REFRESHMENTS	Kranjska Gora (bring sandwiches for the ride)
PARKING	Car park at foot of ski slopes in centre of Kranjska Gora

OVERVIEW

Don't be put off by the relatively large amount of road on this ride. What you have here is a gradual (but stiff) climb out of the ski valley of Kranjska Gora with a fabulous descent to follow. Surrounded by mountains, you make your way up to the south-facing slopes close to the Austrian border with great views back to the town. After a traverse through the woods, you can treat yourself to the 3.5km red descent by the side of the River Jerman. This route is only short, but it packs a lot in.

DIRECTIONS

1 From the car park opposite Sporty Bar, turn ➔ onto the quiet road that traverses the bottom of the resort's ski runs. After about 2km, turn ➔ off

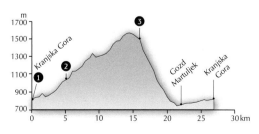

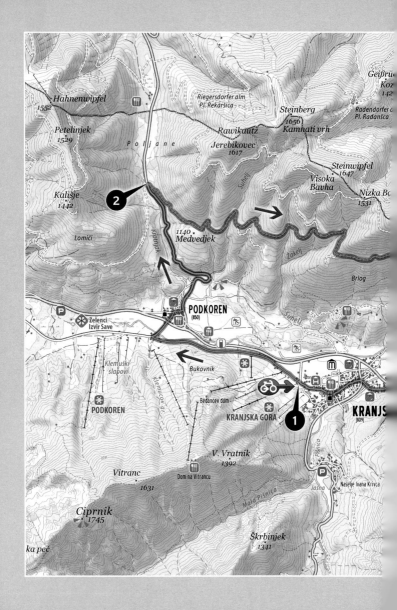

Enjoying one of the best descents in the area

the track at the piste map and then continue ↑ at the crossroads with the main road. This takes you into the quaint little village of **Podkoren**, where you continue ↑ at the crossroads next to the Hotel Vitranc. Turn ← at the T-junction with the main road and follow this, through the hairpin, up to the → at the blue cycle sign for route 9 after about 2km.

❷ After leaving the road behind you, continue climbing on the forest track and at the fork just after a small bridge another 2km further on, keep ←. At the next fork, turn ← again, following the blue sign for route 9. Continue now on the main track for about another 6km until you pass through a green gate (**caution: it's usually closed**). Shortly after the gate, look out for the → signposted *Alpe Adria Trail*; this is the beginning of the lovely descent.

❸ Follow the singletrack as it weaves its way alongside the **River Jerman. This is part of a long-distance walking route and there may be hikers making their way along it too.** The trail eventually spits you out onto a road at **Srednji Vrh**, where you turn ← and head past the farmhouse. At the next fork, head → downhill, following the blue route 10 sign towards **Gozd Martuljek**. After a couple of kilometres of hairpin bends and waterfalls you turn → at the T-junction with the main road, following the sign for *Kranjska Gora*. Just before the steel bridge, look for the **easy-to-miss** ← and then turn → after the smaller bridge. This brings you on to the D-2 cycleway; follow this back to **Kranjska Gora** and the car.

The high meadow of Tolminske Ravne (Route 13)

The Soča Valley

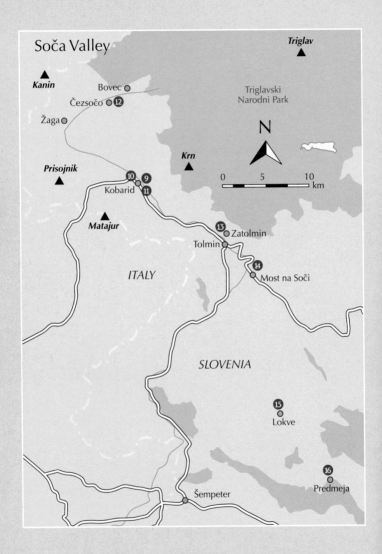

The spectacular River Soča

If Gorenjska is the big brother – mature, sophisticated and stylish – then the Soča Valley is the younger brother addicted to adrenalin sports. This region is the home of adventure sports in Slovenia, most of which are centred around the spectacular River Soča. Natural minerals make the river bright turquoise in colour and it runs from white water rapids to placid lakes, making it a magnet for watersports enthusiasts. From this market has grown a wealth of other outdoor activity providers, including paragliding, climbing and, of course, mountain biking. Needless to say, it's a stunning area with the mountains rising almost sheer from the valley bottom, waterfalls cascading out of them and gorges giving up their secrets to the adventurous.

There are a number of good towns to stay in. Starting at the top, there's Bovec: the home of the outdoor sports. It grew up as a ski resort and retains that alpine party atmosphere. A little further down the valley is Kobarid, the gateway to the Soča mountains. Kobarid is a little more sedate than Bovec but has restaurants, hotels and a lot more history: Kobarid is 'Capodistra', one of the towns in Ernest Hemingway's famous World War 1 novel *A Farewell to Arms*. Finally, as the river slackens and the mountains return to (big) hills, there are the two towns of Tolmin and Most na Soči. Tolmin is the administrative capital of the region and has all the facilities you could need, but is a rather uninspiring town in its own right. However, Most na Soči is much smaller and more quaint; you'd need to travel to get to most things but, if you're looking for somewhere away from the bustle further up the valley, this might be for you.

ACCOMMODATION

Bovec probably has the biggest selection of accommodation, from the newly built Hotel Mangart with its wellness centre to smaller lodges and inns further up the slopes of the mountains. One other option in Bovec is the apartments popular with skiers. Apartments Mavrič (www.apartments-mavric.com/en) are an excellent option. The owner, Bostjan, speaks very good English, is a keen mountain biker himself and maintains a bike workshop in the basement of the apartments.

Kobarid has fewer options for accommodation and the best of those is Hotel Hvala in the centre of town. Again, however, apartments are also available, including Hemingway House – a B&B in a 19th-century house right in the centre of town.

Tolmin has Hotel Krn, which hints at an opulent past at very reasonable prices. In Most na Soči, Hotel Lucija sits next to the eponymous bridge with views of the beautiful lake. It's also designated a *kolesarski* hotel, meaning it has facilities for cyclists and bikers.

SERVICES

There is a tourist information centre in all of the main towns in the area, including Bovec, Kobarid and Tolmin. As with all tourist information centres across Slovenia, they have excellent, English-speaking staff, good maps and region-specific information for bikers.

The towns most suitable for bike hire are Bovec and Kobarid. Bovec has an embarrassment of riches as far as bike shops go, but Outdoor Galaxy (www.outdoor-galaxy.com) do some of the best for reasonable prices. In Kobarid, your best option is probably X-Point Hostel (en.xpoint.si), which is, obviously, also an accommodation option for those on a budget.

EMERGENCIES

There are good health centres and clinics as well as pharmacies in all of the following towns: Bovec, Kobarid and Tolmin.

Route 9
Kobarid and the River Soča

START/FINISH	Main square, Kobarid
DISTANCE	18.5km (11½ miles)
ON ROAD	12km (7½ miles)
OFF ROAD	6.5km (4 miles)
ASCENT	755m (2475ft)
GRADE	▲
TIME	1hr 30min–2hr
MAP	Alpski Svet – Zahodni Del
REFRESHMENTS	Gostišče Jelkin Hram, Drežnica (seasonal) or Kobarid (all year)
PARKING	Plenty of car parks dotted around Kobarid

OVERVIEW

At first sight, this route may not appear to be up to much with its brevity and the high road content. However, if you're in the area and you miss it out, you're denying yourself a little treat. The climb comes at the beginning and then it's downhill virtually all the way, taking in quaint villages and a lovely, wooded descent down to the spectacular Soča River which you then cross and follow most of the way back. At most, this little ride will take a couple of hours: go on, treat yourself.

DIRECTIONS

① Standing in the square with your back to the church, go ↑ and around the right-hand bend. After a very short time, turn → at the fork, following the sign for *Drežnica*. Down the hill you'll come to the fabulous **Napoleon Bridge** high above the turquoise Soča; cross this and turn immediately ←. Follow this road up the mountain for around 4.5km until you reach the tiny town of **Drežnica**.

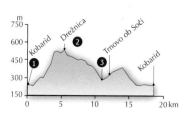

2 At the first fork you come to, turn ←, following signs for *Magozd* and *Jezerca*. At the next fork, in **Jezerca**, again take the ←, following the sign for *Magozd*. Shortly you'll pass through the hillside village of **Magozd**; at the end of the village take the → fork and follow the sign for *Trnovo*. Here you'll lose the road and begin the descent. This lovely little track will take you through woods and meadows all the way down to the river: just turn ← and ← again at the two forks, all the time following signs for *Trnovo*. The final descent to the bridge, about 3km from Magozd, is a singletrack, probably graded red, so **exercise caution**.

3 If you're feeling brave, ride across the gently swinging suspension bridge, but don't forget to stop and admire the river. After the bridge, turn →. Follow the track until it becomes a road and enters the village of **Trnovo ob Soči**. At the church, turn ← and ← again onto the main road. Ride for around 2km and then, at the apex of a **right-hand** bend, look out for the **easy-to-miss** ← out of a parking lay-by, signed for *Napoleonava Pot*. Follow this trail back down to the river (and then alongside it) all the way back to the Napoleon Bridge. From here, return to the centre of **Kobarid** the way you originally came.

The lovely singletrack down to the river near Trnovo

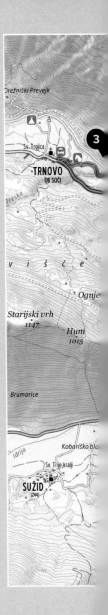

The rather fine Napoleon Bridge near Kobarid

Route 10
Stol epic

START/FINISH	Main square, Kobarid
DISTANCE	59km (36½ miles)
ON ROAD	21km (13 miles)
OFF ROAD	38km (23½ miles)
ASCENT	2205m (7235ft)
GRADE	◆
TIME	5–6hr
MAP	Alpski Svet – Zahodni Del
REFRESHMENTS	Kobarid or Robič (take sandwiches and plenty of water)
PARKING	Plenty of car parks dotted around Kobarid

OVERVIEW

There's no doubt about it, this ride is a beast: at 59km and over 2200m of ascent, it's a big ask of anyone. If, however, you're feeling fit and you've got a full day to play with, it's a classic. It begins and ends in Kobarid, the gateway to the Soča Valley and its course encompasses all that is great about the area. From a long, tough climb through the forest to an 11km descent with great vistas and to the beautiful River Soča itself, this route really has got it all. Whenever the locals hear that you're mountain biking in the area, they always ask, 'Have you done Stol yet?' Now's your chance.

DIRECTIONS

1 Standing in the square with your back to the church, go ↑ and round the **right-hand** bend then take the → fork signed for *Drežnica*. As you approach the **Napoleon Bridge** over the Soča, turn ← off the road just before the bridge itself, heading for Kamp Koren. Follow the trail for around 3km until you meet the main road again and turn → onto it. At the far end of the village of **Trnovo** turn →, following the sign for *Kamp Trnovo*. Follow this road, which becomes a track, down to the suspension bridge over the river and make sure you enjoy the view as you cross.

ŽAGA
(352)
3

Sekeljni

Map continued on page 76

M. Polovnik
1471

V. Polovnik
1476

Pl. Polovnik

Murna glava
1080

m
10

Sušec

Sušec

SRPENICA
Sv. Florijan

Zaglava
930

Brezovo

Banc

Lk

Pl. Pri starih hramih

Treska
646

Stol
1673

Osojnica

Na Verilih

Pl. Božica

M. vrh
1405

Vršanja glava
1368

Na vr
1231

Gošče

b
3

Goštenk

Robušek

STANOVIŠČE

Sv. Katarina

Nova Borjana

BORJANA

POTOKI

Mokar

Hurja

NADIŽA

KRED
(254)

5

PODBELA
(309)

Sv. Volar

Debelo čelo
605

ROBIČ
(246)

Pl. Sp. Mija

Turjeva jama

Jama v Moldniku

Žalostna g

Pl. Zg. Mija

Preval
936

Zgorivec

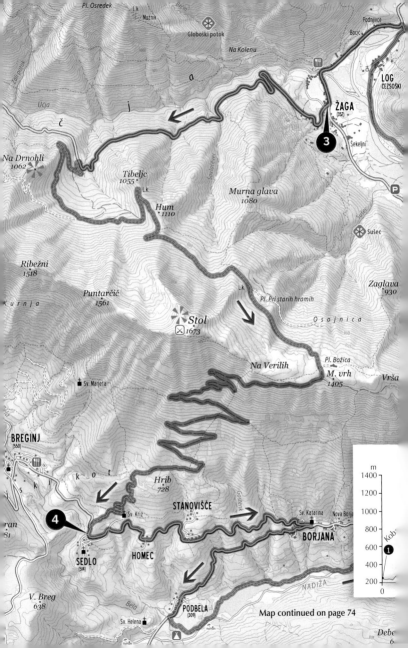

Map continued on page 74

2 After the bridge, turn ←, following the sign for *Log Čezsoški*. Follow the purpose-built off-road bike trail along the spectacular **River Soča**, keeping ← at the next three small junctions. After around 2km go ↑ at the junction with the bridge to the left, again following the sign to *Log Čezsoški*. A further 3km or so further and you'll enter **Log Čezsoški** itself; turn → at the T-junction. Turn ← to cross the river on a road bridge and ← again at the main road, signposted for *Kobarid*. Follow this road, passing through **Žaga**, until you come to a sign in two languages for *Učja/Uccea*; turn → here and prepare for your climb.

Crossing the River Soča

3 The first 5km are on road:
simply keep going until the road flattens out at the top of the pass and you approach the old Slovenian side of the border crossing. Turn ← here just before the defunct passport check onto the very minor road, which quickly becomes a gravel track, following the sign for *Planina Božca* and *Stol*. A little further on, turn ← at the next fork, again following the signs. This track will then take you all the way to the summit plateau at **Na Verilih** over 6km further on. It's a long, tough climb but the views from the top make up for it. As you top out, put on another layer and grab your sandwiches for the most

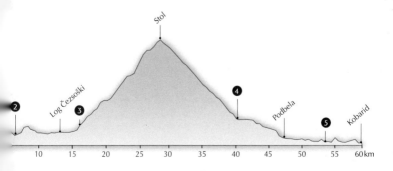

The 11km descent from Stol

spectacular lunch stop in this book. After lunch, at the ridge, turn → and then take the next fork ← to begin your 11km descent. You're welcome.

4 After 18 hairpin bends and dropping 890m you eventually come to a road, where you turn ←. You can, if you're tired, follow this road all the way back to Kobarid, but that would be to miss out on a charming little extension along the Nadiža River. In **Borjana**, turn → at the next junction with the church on the **left**. Follow this road through the village of **Podbela** and turn ← at the sign for *Kamp Nadiža*. At the next T-junction, turn →, following the **Nadiža River**, and from then on follow the blue-and-white cycle signs. At the four-way junction go ↑ and follow this to the swimming hole and café. Turn ← onto the road just after the car park, heading towards Robič.

5 Turn → off this road just before a roundabout sign about 1km further along. Follow this track to the village of **Sužid** and go ↑ through it. Again, follow the blue-and-white cycle signs heading towards Svino until you come to a T-junction with the road, then turn ←. Turn ← again at the next T-junction and follow this road back to the church in **Kobarid**.

Route 11

Kobarid and the River Nadiža

START/FINISH	Main square, Kobarid
DISTANCE	14.5km (9 miles)
ON ROAD	5km (3 miles)
OFF ROAD	9.5km (6 miles)
ASCENT	325m (1065ft)
GRADE	■
TIME	1hr 30min–2hr
MAP	Alpski Svet – Zahodni Del
REFRESHMENTS	Kobarid (all year), Robič (in season)
PARKING	Plenty of car parks dotted around Kobarid

OVERVIEW

Take a break from the high mountains all around you and have a gentle day pedalling through beautiful river meadows. This route, beginning and ending in the historical centre of Kobarid is a gentle exploration of the Nadiža valley. Running along a disused railway bed and the river itself, you'll encounter farming communities, swimming holes and spectacular vistas of the mountains. It's not always all about the downhill.

DIRECTIONS

1 From the main square, with your back to the church, turn → and very shortly afterwards turn → again at the sign for *Svino*. Turn → and then immediately ←, following the sign for *Nadiža* – you're now following the blue-and-white bicycle signs. At the next fork turn → and this will bring you to the little community of **Sužid**; at the crossroads go ↑, following the sign for *Kolesarska Pot Nadiža*. When you reach the road, turn → onto it.

2 Just a couple of hundred metres along the road you'll come to a roundabout; take the third exit, signposted for *Breginj* and *Podbela*. A further 200m later, turn ← off this road just before the *Breginjski Pot* sign. Follow this track through the meadows until you come to a road at **Kred** and turn →. Turn ← off this road almost straight away, following the sign for *Reki Nadiži*. At the next fork turn ← again, following the blue bike sign, and follow this trail down to the **Nadiža River** where you turn ← to follow it, crossing a ford along the way. Take time on this stretch to stop and appreciate the beauty of the river before arriving at the swimming hole and restaurant at **Robič**.

Taking it easy along the valley bottom

3 At the road just after the restaurant's car park, turn ←. This road returns you to beginning of the old rail bed that leads, through Sužid, back to Kobarid. Just before the roundabout sign, turn → off this road and onto the track. Follow this track for round 5km, retracing your outward route, back to **Kobarid**.

Crossing the ford near to the River Nadiža

On the sweeping upper descent from Stol

Route 12
Stol and the long descent

START/FINISH	Hotel Ana, 5km south-west of Bovec
DISTANCE	37km (23 miles)
ON ROAD	10km (6¼ miles)
OFF ROAD	27km (16¾ miles)
ASCENT	1660m (5445ft)
GRADE	◆
TIME	4–5hr
MAP	Alpski Svet – Zahodni Del
REFRESHMENTS	Bovec (take sandwiches and plenty of water)
PARKING	Behind Hotel Ana

75%
OFF ROAD

OVERVIEW

Compared with the route from Kobarid, this may seem the easier option for climbing Stol – but don't be deceived. Certainly, it's a shorter route, but that climb is still as tough. The thing that ups the ante on this ride is the descent. At over 12km it'll test your endurance, and it will also test your skill: the initial sweeping descent becomes a technical black drop, with a hair-raising section along a knife-edge arête. Not for the faint-hearted if you're planning to ride it all, but those with a healthier sense of self-preservation can walk the really technical sections.

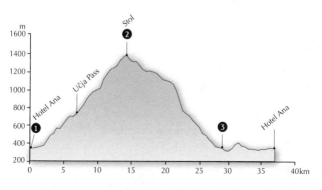

Directions

1 From the car park, turn ← onto the busy main road and continue for 2km. As you enter the village of **Žaga**, turn → up the hill, signposted for *Učja/Uccea*. This is the beginning of your long climb. After around 5km, at

Finally cresting the rise at Stol

the plateau with the old border crossing, turn ←. At the next fork, again go ←, following the sign for *Planina Stol*. Continue all the way to the summit plateau at **Na Verilih**.

2 As you finally crest the rise, look back over your shoulder to admire the mountains and then keep ↑ to drop down onto the ridge. Turn ← and begin your fabulous descent, making the most of the fast-flowing start. As you drop down to a saddle with a four-way sign, keep ↑ and battle briefly up the slope on the other side to the viewpoint at **Na Vrhu**. As you start to descend again, this is the beginning of the black run. When you finally drop out of the woods shortly after passing through **Hum**, keep ↑ up the short slope and then turn → onto the gravel track downhill.

3 At the T-junction with the main road, turn ←. In **Trnovo ob Soči**, turn → after the church, signposted for *Kamp Trnovo*. Cross the suspension bridge over the spectacular **River Soča** and turn ←. At the next fork, keep ←, following the sign for *Alpe Adria Trail*, and continue for around 6km until you come to the village of **Log Čezsoški**. Keep ↑ and then turn → at the T-junction. Turn ← over the bridge and back to the car park.

Route 13
Planina Razor

Start/Finish	Tolminke Gorge car park, Zatolmin
Distance	35km (21¾ miles)
On road	22.5km (14 miles)
Off road	12.5km (7¾ miles)
Ascent	2100m (6890ft)
Grade	▲
Time	4–5hr
Map	Alpski Svet – Zahodni Del
Refreshments	Koča Planini Razor (every day July–Sep, weekends May, June and Oct)

Overview

Don't be put off by the quantity of road on this ride; it's the quality of the off-road that you undertake this route for. There is well over 4km of fabulous red-grade singletrack coming off the summit of this beautiful mountain. You also get the opportunity to explore the famous cheese dairies on the way up. The initial climb out of Ljubinj is tough but the rest is easy angled, all the way to the Razor plateau

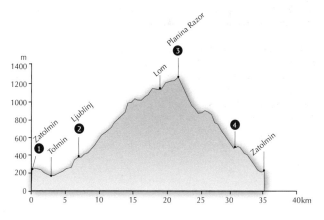

itself and the stunning vista out to the Soča Valley. But really, I can't recommend that downhill enough.

DIRECTIONS

1 The Tolminke Gorge is spectacular and worth a visit if you have the time. However, from the car park, head through **Zatolmin** back towards Tolmin. Once you reach **Tolmin**, turn ← at the crossroads in the centre. As you climb up and leave the town, turn ← at the sign for *Poljubinj* and *Ljubinj* and follow this road, going through **Poljubinj**, for around 4km. In **Ljubinj**, just after the church, turn ← at the sign for *Planina Razor* and begin the climb in earnest.

2 The climb begins steeply; keep going until you reach a fork about 8km after leaving Ljubinj and go ↑ (if you turn R you can visit the other mountain restaurant on this route at **Stador**). The angle of the slope eases here. Pass through the little village of **Lom**, following signs for *Koča Planini Razor*. Follow this track for about 3.5km through the cheesery at **Kuk** all the way to the plateau at **Razor** and the restaurant.

This route features one of the finest singletracks in Slovenia

Just outside Tolminske Ravne

❸ When you're ready for the descent, take the ← just before the hut, signposted *Tolminske Ravne*. The trail passes below and parallel to the track you came up on. This is the beginning of about 3km of singletrack through beech forest. When you come to the village of **Tolminske Ravne**, about 4km from Razor, pass through the gate and turn → at the road. As you head down, count the hairpin bends. After the seventh (a left-hander), look out for the **easy-to-miss** → about 50m further down, signposted *Tolmin*.

❹ Take the turn and head down the second of the sections of singletrack. This one is shorter but more of an adventure; be prepared to carry the bike past a stream at one point. As you drop out of the woods at **Zadlaz**, turn ← at the T-junction with the concrete road. At the next junction (signs for *Čadrg* and *Zadlaz*) turn ← downhill. Follow this road over the gorge and back to the **car park**.

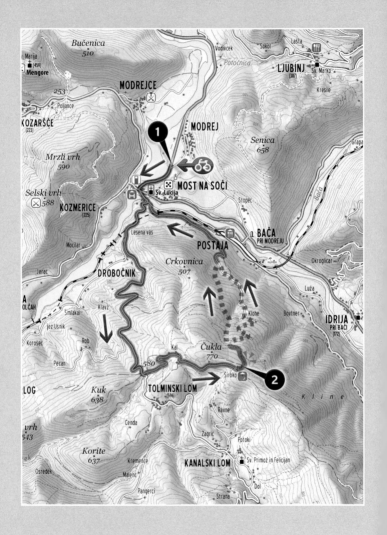

Route 14
Most na Soči Široko

14

START/FINISH	Lakeside car park, Most na Soči
DISTANCE	12km (7½ miles)
ON ROAD	7km (4½ miles)
OFF ROAD	5km (3 miles)
ASCENT	720m (2360ft)
GRADE	▲/◆
TIME	1–1hr 30min
MAP	Alpski Svet – Zahodni Del
REFRESHMENTS	Most na Soči (all year)
PARKING	Most na Soči is a small place and parking in the centre is limited. Instead, take the road towards Tolmin and on the right, next to the lake is a bigger car park.

40% OFF ROAD

OVERVIEW

It's a short but sweet route out of the quaint little lakeside town of Most na Soči up to the heights of Široko and down again. The climb is a bit stiff but blessedly brief, and the views from the tourist farm at the summit are truly marvellous. However, it is the downhill where this route comes alive, with the option of either a leisurely (yet steep) descent through the hairpins and meadows or a straighter line down through the local bike park. Be warned: the latter option is really only for those with full-sus bikes with plenty of travel.

DIRECTIONS

1 From the parking, turn ← back into town. At the T-junction in town, take the almost hidden road, ↑ down the hill and over the bridge, then follow the road → up the hill and through **Dobročnik**. Keep climbing until your first ← as it flattens out, signposted for *Turistična Kmetija Široko*. Follow

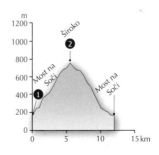

All the places you could go from the summit of Široko

this little lane, through **Kal**, all the way to the tourist farm at the summit of **Široko**.

2 Take time to admire the views and photograph yourself at the swan sculpture bench, then head down the track next to the farm buildings. At the first hairpin you have a choice: 1) follow the track → for the easier descent, or 2) take the metre-high drop-off to the ← and enter the downhill park. Either way, the route will bring you down to a concrete track just above **Postaja**. As you approach the bottom you'll hear the road; on the final **right-hand** hairpin, turn off ←. After just over 1km this will bring you back down to **Most na Soči** and the little bridge you crossed near the start. Re-trace your route back to the car park.

Route 15

The war memorial at Trnovo

START/FINISH	Village centre, Lokve
DISTANCE	22km (13½ miles)
ON ROAD	10km (6 miles)
OFF ROAD	12km (7½ miles)
ASCENT	350m (1150ft)
GRADE	■
TIME	1hr 30min–2hr
MAP	Primorska
REFRESHMENTS	Lokve and Trnovo (all year)
PARKING	Car park behind bar opposite bus stop

OVERVIEW

This gently undulating route will take you through forests ruled by bear, lynx and wolf (although, to be honest, you'll be lucky to see any of them). It's not a tough ride, taking place, as it does, on forest tracks and asphalt roads; however, you'll pass a pleasant morning or afternoon in an area that's largely ignored by tourists. Most importantly, you'll also have the opportunity to explore the dramatic war memorial at Trnovo.

DIRECTIONS

1 Facing the bus stop, turn ← out of the car park and follow the road downhill, heading towards Nova Gorica. Turn → off the road onto the forest track at the small war memorial. At the first fork (about 2km further on),

The names of all of Slovenia's fallen line the stairs of the memorial near Trnovo

Gently undulating forest trails await you

take the ➜ and then
follow the main track
downhill all the way
to **Zavrh**. As you get to
the tarmac just after the
house on the **right**, turn
←.

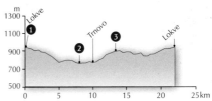

2 Follow this road for 4km through high pastures and eventually down to
the famous and impressive war memorial, Spominski Park Nob. Take time
to lock the bikes up and have a look around here before returning to the
route. At the T-junction, turn ← (if you're coming from Lokve) and follow
this road towards **Trnovo**. Take the ➜ just before reaching the town and go
↑ when you then reach the main road. Shortly after, take the next ← at the
crossroads. Follow this road for around 4km through the village of **Rijavci**
and on into the birch forest. At the second forest track on the **left**, turn ←.

3 Ignore the first track that comes in from the **right** and continue for around
2.5km. Then, at the road, turn ➜ then immediately ➜ again just before the
dead-end sign. At the next T-junction, turn ← and follow this track down to
the road at **Nemci**. Turn ➜ and then, after the last house on the **left**, turn ←
onto the forest track. At the next T-junction turn ➜ and follow your outward
route back to the car park at **Lokve**.

Birch and limestone: typical of this Karst landscape

Route 16

The dark forests of Trnovo

90% OFF ROAD

START/FINISH	Mala Lazna junction (near the bikers' inn)
DISTANCE	29km (18 miles)
ON ROAD	3.5km (2¼ miles)
OFF ROAD	25.5km (15¾ miles)
ASCENT	925m (3035ft)
GRADE	■
TIME	2–3hr
MAP	Primorska
REFRESHMENTS	Koča Antona Bavčerja (Friday to Sunday, all year)
PARKING	Roadside at Mala Lazna

OVERVIEW

The forests of the Karst Plateau around Trnovo are full of legend. They're also full of animals, including three top predators. This route does have a bit of climbing in it but it's essentially a gentle roll around these dark and exciting forests. There's an opportunity to visit an ice cave (velika ledena jama) from which ice used to be shipped all the way to Egypt. You'll also pass along the southern edge of the plateau which, on a good day, offers views out over the Vipava Valley as far as the Adriatic coast.

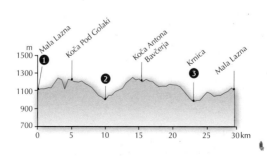

Emerging from the murk on an unusually inclement day on the way down from the second of the two mountain huts

DIRECTIONS

1 From the large flat area around the junction, head north-east along the track signposted *Ledenica*. Begin climbing here and, after around 2km, look out for the little footpath down to the **ice cave** on the **right**. Just after the ice cave, at the T-junction, turn **→**. A little way along here, you'll come to a large open area with an option to walk to the first of two mountain huts, **Iztokova Koča pod Golaki**.

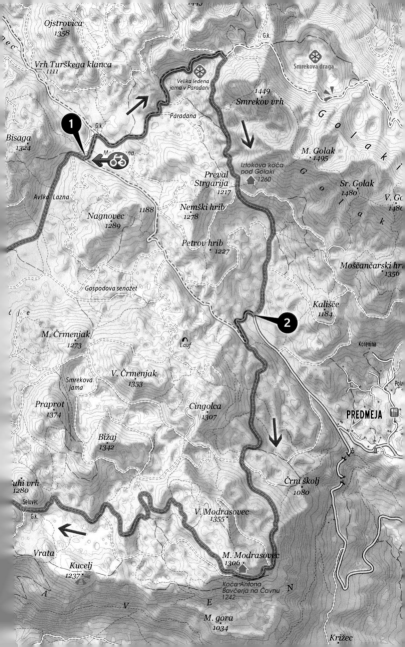

If you decide not to, follow the track around to the ←. Begin descending, and at the T-junction turn ←.

2 At the next T-junction, turn → to start climbing again. At the apex of the next hairpin, turn ←, following the sign for *Koča na Čavnu*. This is the last tough climb and will bring you, in 4km, to the second hut, **Koča Antona Bavčerja na Čavnu**, and some great views off the southern edge of the plateau. Behind the restaurant, take the → fork. At the next T-junction turn ←, and at the one after that turn →. After a little less than 5km, this will eventually bring you down to the tiny village of **Krnica** (three houses and a maypole).

3 At the T-junction in front of the orange house, turn →, and when the road begins, follow it round to the →. The road lasts for around 1.5km; shortly after it finishes at the next T-junction, next to the information board, turn ← and then ← again at the next one. From here it's around 3km, heading downhill, back to the car at **Mala Lazna**.

Crossing the River Idrijca (Route 17)

The South

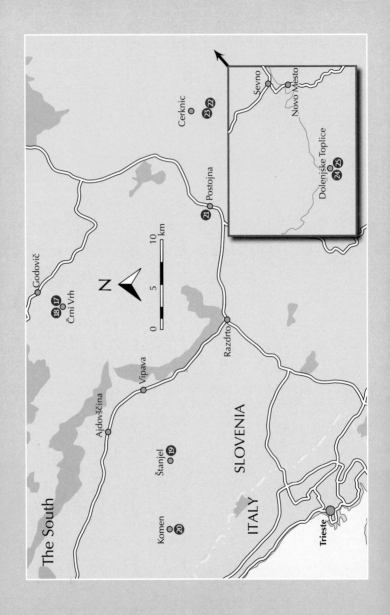

The South

ITALY

SLOVENIA

Trieste

Komen ● 20

Štanjel ● 19

Ajdovščina ●

Vipava ●

Razdrto ●

Črni Vrh 18 17

Godovič ●

Postojna ● 21

N

0 5 10 km

Cerknic ● 23 22

Sevno

Novo Mesto

Dolenjske Toplice 24 25

The war memorial on the trail to Kostanjevica is one of many in this frontline region

Strictly speaking, 'the south' isn't really a region in its own right. The area I've designated in this book as the south (everything below a gently curving line from Nova Gorica to Novo Mesto) is, in actual fact, composed of many different regions and landscapes. To the north there is the Karst: a limestone shield riddled with caves and cloaked in forest. To the east, near the border with Croatia, the hills flatten out, becoming more undulating, and you get the chance to stay in thermal spring resorts. Finally, although this book doesn't list any rides right down in the south, while you're in the area you may as well pop along to the coast and soak up the Mediterranean-style atmosphere.

The rides for this section are clustered in three areas: around the towns of Ajdovščina, Postojna and Novo Mesto. Ajdovščina is an old Roman city built at the foot of the Karst shield. Much of the town's history, including most of its old walls, has been preserved. It is also the largest of the Vipava Valley towns and, therefore, has the most in the way of accommodation and shopping. That said, I prefer the smaller, quieter and equally ancient town of Vipava for my accommodation when I'm in the area. Postojna has been a tourist town since the Victorian period, when visitors poured in from the Hapsburg empire to marvel at the caves and culture. It still retains that touristic lure and, even if you don't stay here, is worth a visit just for the spectacular caves and the famous Predjama Grad: a castle in the mouth of a cave halfway up a cliff. Finally Novo Mesto is not, as its name suggests, a new town, having been founded in 1365. Its Old Town is almost entirely surrounded by water, sitting as it does in the crook of a bend in the River Krka. The aerial photographs are spectacular and it's definitely worth a look at street-level too.

ACCOMMODATION

In Ajdovščina, one of your better options for accommodation is the Hotel Gold Club (hotelgoldclub.eu), which, whilst having a slightly alarming name, does actually provide a very comfortable standard at reasonable prices. It also has a very pleasant restaurant and a bar. Also in town there is a youth hostel for those on a budget (www.youth-hostel.si).

Postojna has a plethora of options if you're thinking of staying there. Top of the list for any biker should be Hotel Sport (www.epiceco-hotels.com), which is a designated *kolesarski* (cycle-friendly) hotel with fabulous amenities for mountain bikers and cyclists alike. They are also the first port of call for any further information about mountain biking in the area. For those on a tighter budget, just out of town (but on two of the routes in this guide) is Camping Pivka Jama (camping-postojna.com/en). All the facilities you'd expect are there, and in addition there's a very reasonable restaurant, bungalows can be rented and it even has its own cave to explore.

The Old Town of Novo Mesto, as you might expect, doesn't have many accommodation options. There is the hostel Situla (www.situla.si/en) right in the thick of it, but the better options are out of town a little, where you can find the thermal bath resorts. Operated by Terme Krka (www.terme-krka.com/us/en, then click on 'destinations'), there are a few options but I personally recommend the ones in the wooded seclusion of Doljenske Toplice, where they also have a member of staff dedicated to helping mountain bikers.

SERVICES

Postojna is easily the best place to hire a bike or get one serviced. There are plenty of options here, but your first port of call should probably be the Hotel Sport. In addition, bikes can be hired from the Terme Krka hotels in and around Novo Mesto but the quality is not as good.

Once again, the tourist information centres in the towns of Ajdovščina, Vipava, Postojna, Cernikca (just to the east of Postojna) and Novo Mesto all have very useful information and specially printed biking maps.

EMERGENCIES

There are good health centres and clinics as well as pharmacies in all of the following towns: Ajdovščina, Postojna, Cerknica and Novo Mesto.

Route 17
The industrial heritage of Črni Vrh

START/FINISH	Village centre, Črni Vrh
DISTANCE	48km (30 miles)
ON ROAD	15km (9½ miles)
OFF ROAD	33km (20½ miles)
ASCENT	1915m (6280ft)
GRADE	▲
TIME	3–4hr
MAP	Primorska
REFRESHMENTS	Idrijska Bela
PARKING	Mercator supermarket

70%
OFF ROAD

OVERVIEW

A varied route that will not only give you a great experience of the classic lime-stone geology of the Kras landscape (after which karst is named) but which will also open a window onto the region's early industrial past. The ride reveals, among other things, a giant, peaceful sinkhole fed by one of the shortest rivers in Europe, as well as mill leats and the 'Slovenian Pyramids': dams built by char-coal loggers to wash the trees downstream to the markets. It does have some stiff climbs but the landscape and history make them more than worth it.

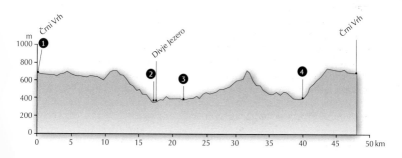

Directions

❶ From the supermarket car park, opposite the church, turn ➜ onto the road. After less than a kilometre you'll pass a **petrol station**; around 1km further on, look out for the small roadside shrine next to a **right** turn and turn ← across the field. When you reach the village of **Predgriže**, follow the track around to the **left** and keep ↑ for around 3km. When you reach the road, turn ➜, aiming for Idrijska Log. Around 1.5km later, turn ← at a small cluster of buildings. This is now the long, thin village of **Idrijski Log**; just at the end of the village, turn ➜. After entering the woods, turn ➜ onto the old railway

A section of singletrack on the hilly Karst terrain

track-bed that is now a singletrack. Follow this lovely trail for around 3.5km along the edge of the hill to the next fork and take the ←. The trail ends at a gate and a T-junction where you turn ←. Follow this now down the hill, through the eleven hairpin bends and eventually out to the road.

2 The tricky navigating is now done. Turn ← onto the road and follow this a short distance and then, just before you cross the bridge that spans the short river, turn ←. Dismount and walk the very short distance to **Divje Jezero**, the sinkhole lake which is quite impressive. Return to the bridge and continue the way you were travelling. At the footbridge on the **right**, turn → to cross it and then immediately ← to follow the mill leat. This path becomes a singletrack; follow it, using the **Idrijca River** on the **left** as a handrail, until you come to a fork. Turn ← towards the road. At the road, turn →. It's possible to get refreshments here but if you're not yet hungry, don't worry, you'll be passing back this way in about 17km time. A little further on, at the junction of two rivers, take the ← fork.

3 Follow this track now along the river and up the hill. Along the way are the 'Slovenian Pyramids': impressive-looking dams that were built to back up enough water to sluice felled trees back down to Idrija. Take some time to explore them. Continuing, after about 1.5km you'll come to the junction at **Krekovše**; turn ← (although there is a great view a short way to the right). About 300m later, just after some huts, turn → and then → again at the next fork a further 700m further on, heading downhill. The descent is now a lovely, flowing and easy run on the Idrijski 'lauf' (Idija Railway). After around 2km, at the T-junction just after the bridge, turn →, and then → again at the next T-junction a kilometre further on. Eventually this brings you out at the junction of the two rivers you passed earlier; here turn ←. Follow the road now and back over the bridge with the restaurant. Immediately after this, turn →, following the sign for *Zadlog*.

4 At the next fork, turn ←, again following the sign for *Zadlog*. A further 3km of climbing will bring you to another fork; again turn ←. At the next opportunity, turn ← following the sign for *Zadlog*. At the staggered crossroads at **Šoštar**, go ↑ and follow this road to the main road where you'll see your car park ahead of you in **Črni Vrh**.

The beautiful sinkhole lake, Divje Jezero

Route 18
Javornik

Start/Finish	Village centre, Črni Vrh
Distance	21.5km (13¼ miles)
On road	6.5km (4 miles)
Off road	15km (9¼ miles)
Ascent	1035m (3395ft)
Grade	▲
Time	1hr 30min–2hr 30min
Map	Primorska
Refreshments	Pirnatova Koča (weekends)
Parking	Mercator supermarket

Overview

The Nanos plateau and the peaks that stick up out of it provide some fabulous views. This route, beginning in Črni Vrh, climbs up to that plateau and on to the ski centre at Javornik. There is a bike park here in the non-winter months and this route includes some of the downhill singletrack that makes this proposition so much fun. It's only short, but you'll get your share of climbing, vistas and descents on this cheeky half-day out.

Directions

1 From the car park, turn ← and almost immediately begin your ascent on the road. About 5.5km later, turn ← at the sign for *Javornik*. After 400m turn ← onto the next gravel track and follow this to a fork, where you turn ← uphill. At the next fork, turn ← again and then → uphill at the following fork. Shortly after this turning, you'll come to a saddle just before a

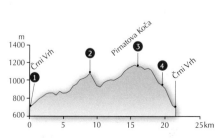

building; dismount here and follow the footpath off to the ← for a great view out over Črni Vrh.

❷ Back on the track, continue ↑ through the grounds of the farmhouse and uphill, following the walking path signs. At the T-junction, turn ← (dismounting and heading right here would, after a short walk, bring you out to another spectacular view). At the next T-junction turn ← again, heading downhill until you come out of the trees and to the next T-junction. Turn → and take the ← fork immediately afterwards. Follow this trail for around 3.5km and then, after passing underneath the ski lift, take the → fork. You are now in the bike park on the slopes of **Javornik**. Turn → just before the next house, crossing the fence line and heading straight up the hill. At the T-junction turn → and then, at the fork, turn ←, heading downhill. Just after the building, follow the sign for *Pirnatova Koča* ↑. Even if the **hut** isn't open

The view of Črni Vrh is worth taking a moment for

and you've brought your own sandwiches, it's still worth the diversion here to the right for the view alone.

On a clear day you can see the sea from the hut

❸ Heading back down the track from the hut, your descent is the singletrack that heads off to the →. At the crossroads about 600m further on go ↑ and then, at the T-junction, turn → followed by a → (uphill) at the next fork. Very shortly after this you'll come to a hairpin bend; take the (**easy-to-miss**) ← off the apex of the bend onto the singletrack. Enjoy this easy-angled but fun descent, but look out for the → turn about 1km later (there is a red-and-white roundel about 20m down this trail). Again, follow this singletrack until you pop out of the trees and then go ↑ at the crossroads, following the sign for Črni Vrh. This will bring you down to a junction you passed earlier; now go ↑ on the gravel road.

❹ Around 300m after this junction, take the **easy-to-miss** → onto the small trail just after the little shrine. This is the beginning of a lovely section of technical singletrack. Less then a kilometre later, look out for the → turn at the sign for Črni Vrh – 15min. Then, at the crossroads, go ↑ following the trail back down to the road. Turn → onto the road and follow this back into **Črni Vrh** and the car park.

The wine of this region is rightly prized

Route 19
The Wine Region of Kras

19

START/FINISH	Road 204 just west of Kobdilj
DISTANCE	31.5km (19½ miles)
ON ROAD	12.5km (7¾ miles)
OFF ROAD	19km (11¾ miles)
ASCENT	705m (2315ft)
GRADE	■
TIME	1hr 30min–2hr 30min
MAP	Primorska
REFRESHMENTS	Gostilna Tomaj, Tomaj (all year except Wednesdays)
PARKING	Roadside parking on 204 (dir Dutovlje) outside Kobdilj

60%
OFF ROAD

OVERVIEW

Easily one of the top five routes in this guide, this little ride will take you on a lovely adventure through the vineyards. It begins with a gentle climb through a peaceful valley, then plunges into little-used tracks that seem to alternate between forest and vineyard. This is one of the foremost wine-growing regions in Slovenia and there's definitely more of a Mediterranean feel to this area; everything is easy-going – even the climbing. Some of the tracks become a bit indistinct in places, but that just adds to the sense of adventure. It's not technical but you will love it.

DIRECTIONS

1 From the parking, turn **←** and head back towards the village, taking the **→** signposted for *Ajdovščina* and *Vipava*. Follow the road downhill through the

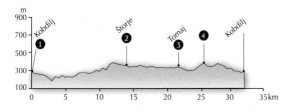

Leaving Štorje: some of the trails here have a very adventurous feel

sweeping bends to a **left-hand** hairpin and turn → off it onto the gravel track. At the T-junction, turn → to stay in the flat Raša River valley. After another kilometre, and after passing through **Mahinči**, turn ← onto the gravel track just before the bridge. Continue for around 5km to the T-junction with the road near to Griže, then turn → and begin the climb up to the plateau. This is the toughest climb all day. After the climb, follow the road for about 1.5km to the next T-junction, where you turn ← and then go ↑ at the crossroads, following the sign for *Pokopališče*. Pass the church and turn → at the playground, bringing you down to a main road at **Štorje**.

2 Go ↑ across this road and then immediately → behind the orange house. The road ends and the track begins at a fork with the village's bins; take the ← fork here. Follow this track, past the business of Prenova, for around 2.5km (it becomes quite indistinct in places), all the way to a T-junction with the road in **Grahovo Brdo**. At this road, turn → and then → again just before the playground. At the next fork, turn ← and then turn ← onto the track when you reach a vineyard on your **right**. Follow this track (again, indistinct in places) to the road at **Utovlje** in sight of the church and turn →. Take this road to the T-junction and take the track ↑ into the woods. After around 500m take the ← fork and then, 100m later at the three-way junction, take the middle route. Follow this for about another 1km all the way to the road at **Tomaj**.

③ The route skirts around Tomaj, so if you want to stop at the *gostilna* (restaurant) here, turn left at the road. Otherwise, turn → and at the next T-junction turn → again. Just 100m later take a further → downhill onto the gravel track. Shortly afterwards, take the → fork and then, immediately, the ← fork. Follow the main trail through the woods (there is one fork that might confuse; head ← in this case) for around 2.5km all the way to the crossroads. Go ↑, following the sign for *Avber*, and follow the road round to the → at the village sign. Keep following the road up through **Avber** and turn ← at Old Rusty, the Harley Davidson fire engine (no really). Head up to the onion-domed **church** at the top of the village.

④ From the church, take the route downhill just behind it (↑ as you approach the church) and into the vineyards. Ignore the first left and then, at the fork among the vines, bear →. Follow this track towards Nova Vas for about a kilometre, and then at the next fork keep ↑, bearing slightly ←. Enjoy this final 3km trail through the woods and when you reach the road, turn →. At the next T-junction turn → again, heading towards Nova Gorica, and follow this road back to the parking area near **Kobdilj**.

The Turk Homestead just outside Tomaj: tempting though it might be, don't stop at all of the wine cellars on the way!

The leafy and tranquil village centre of Kobjeglava

Route 20
Komen and its surrounds

20

START/FINISH	Tuš supermarket, Komen
DISTANCE	52km (32¼ miles)
ON ROAD	15.5km (9½ miles)
OFF ROAD	36.5km (22¾ miles)
ASCENT	1315m (4315ft)
GRADE	▲
TIME	4–5hr
MAP	Primorska
REFRESHMENTS	Stjenkova Koča na Trstelju (all year, Friday to Sunday)
PARKING	At the supermarket

OVERVIEW

This is a tougher prospect than Route 19. We still have the vineyards and the Mediterranean feel, but now we also have a couple of stiff climbs, a bit of difficult navigation and, of course, it's 52km long. It is, however, a lovely day out among the rolling hills and a lot of the riding is on beautifully groomed, purpose-built cycle trails. Take plenty of water, allow yourself the whole day, revel in the smells and enjoy the heat then treat yourself, at the end of the day, to a glass of Refošk and some seafood.

DIRECTIONS

1 From the supermarket car park, enter the town square and take the road to Sežana. Just after the sign indicating the end of town, turn ← onto the gravel trail. After 2km, turn → at the orange cycle sign indicating *Coljava 1km*. As you meet the road in **Coljava** at the crossroads, go ↑ following the orange sign for *Kobjeglava*. This brings you to a small square at TK Ostrouška; keep ↑ up the side of the building and onto the gravel. At the next T-junction, turn → then keep on the main track all the way to a crossroads in the tracks. Turn ←, following the orange sign for *Kobjeglava*, and follow this for about 2.5km all the way to the road at **Kobjeglava**.

Map continued on page 127

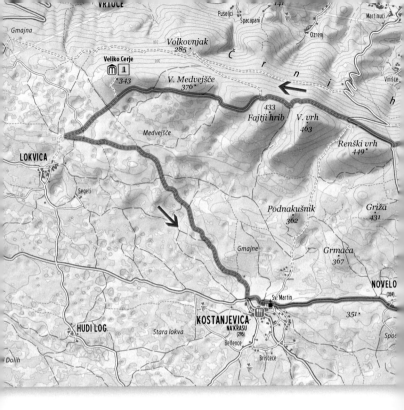

❷ At the five-way junction in Kobjeglava go ↑ (follow the orange sign, weirdly, for Kobjeglava) and then follow the road round through the village and below the church. The road becomes a track; at the shrine take the → fork. About 300m later, at the staggered crossroads, go ↑. Take the → fork 1km further on (again, with the orange sign) and

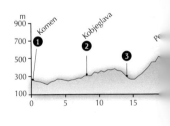

continue for one more kilometre to the T-junction. Turn ←, following the sign for *Lukovec*, and then immediately go ↑. As you enter the open grassland, take the ← fork away from the village of Lukovec and towards Škrbina. Keep

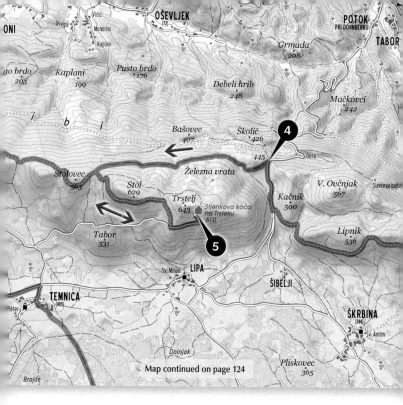

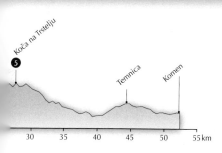

on this trail until you come to barriers across it and private signs almost 2km further on. Ignore these and pass through to the road on the other side. Follow the road to a small T-junction where you turn ←; this takes you down to the main road around 3km from Lukovec.

3 At the T-junction with the main road, turn → downhill. At the apex of the first hairpin bend, turn ← following the sign towards *Pedrovo*. Follow the road into **Pedrovo** and out the other side, where it becomes a track which

you follow for almost a kilometre. At the T-junction in the woods, turn ←
and continue until you shortly come to the next T-junction where you turn
→, continuing uphill. After 500m this brings you to a crossroads on the
ridge; turn → here, following the orange sign for *Sv. Katarina*. Pass the turn-
off for Sv. Katarina and, at the next fork, continue ← downhill. At the road,
turn → and then turn ← off the road just before the little shrine, following
the sign for *Trstelj*.

④ This little section has some tricky navigation. From the turn-off continue to
the next fork out in the open, where you head →, then look out for the **easy-
to-miss** → about 500m further on. This turning is indistinct (as is the trail),
but it is just before the track you're on ramps up and there's a post with a
green trail symbol on it. If you carry on rather than taking this turn, the track
is steep and loose but is a shorter route to the top of Trstelj. If you manage
the turn, you are now on a singletrack overgrown with grass (grass alley);
follow it to the end where it meets the forest track and turn ←. Along this
next section is where you'd come out (from the left) if you took the steep,
loose shortcut. Follow the main track to a T-junction, where you turn ← at
the sign for the *Koča*. The track becomes a road and brings you up to the hut
(**Stjenkova Koča na Trstelju**), which is open at weekends.

⑤ From the hut, retrace your route back to the exit from grass alley and
continue on the track downhill. After just over 4km from the hut, at the
T-junction with the road turn →, and then, at the first hairpin, turn ← onto
the gravel. After about a kilometre, turn → at the red route sign. At the next
T-junction turn →, following the sign for *Cerje*. This track will bring you out
at the car park for **Veliko Cerjo**. This large, castle-like memorial is worth
the diversion for a visit. Having visited, continue downhill on the road.
About 1km further on, turn ← back on yourself (look for the hidden sign for
Kostanjevica). After another kilometre, take the → fork (again following the
sign for *Kostanjevica*) and then, when you reach the road, take a hard ←
(pass the recycling bins on your **right**). At the T-junction with the road, turn
←, pass the **church** and then turn ← again at the next T-junction. Follow
the road for about 2.5km, through the village of **Novelo**, and then turn →
at the sign for Temnica. In the village of **Temnica** itself, turn ← at the stop
sign and then, when you reach the war memorial, turn →, following the sign
for *Vinogradništvo Škaber-Ščuka*. This road becomes a track; follow it for a
lovely 3km to the end and turn ← onto the road. Follow this road all the way
back to the car park at **Komen**.

Route 21

Postojna classic

START/FINISH	Mercator supermarket, west of Postojna town centre
DISTANCE	31km (19¼ miles)
ON ROAD	19km (11¾ miles)
OFF ROAD	12km (7½ miles)
ASCENT	575m (1885ft)
GRADE	■
TIME	2hr 30min–3hr 30min
MAP	Notranjski Kras, Brkini, Dolenjska, Bela Krajina
REFRESHMENTS	Predjama (all year)
PARKING	At the supermarket

OVERVIEW

This is a fabulous route. It takes in some of the very best parts of the region, from the caves of Postojna and Pivka to the castle-in-a-cave at Predjama Grad. Beginning and ending in the tourist town of Postojna, the route is relatively flat (undulating at worst) and takes you through dairy meadows and ancient forests, across the Karst shield and along a river floodplain. You can have lunch overlooking the 13th-century castle (look out for the privy in which the original owner met his fate) and there's even a short section of red-grade singletrack thrown in for good measure. If you want the perfect taste of this area in one bite, then this is the route for you.

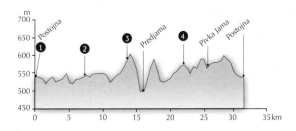

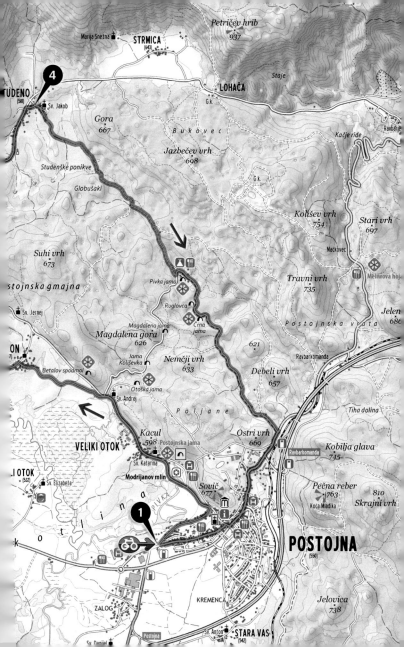

Predjama Grad is one of the most iconic views in Slovenia

Directions

1 From the car park, go ↑ at the first roundabout (the second exit) and follow the signs for the *Jama* (cave) through the next T-junction, where you turn ←. About 1.5km after passing the **Postojna Cave** complex, turn ← off the road opposite another road to Pivka Jama. After about 1km, this track becomes a road and bends 90 degrees to the right in the village of **Zagon**; turn ← here (effectively going straight on down the hill). Go ↑ when this road again becomes a dirt track, and then at the next fork a few hundred metres further on, turn ←. Follow this track for a couple of kilometres all the way to the road.

2 Just before this road there is a track that runs parallel to it; turn → onto it, following the sign for cycle route 2. Turn → onto the next road, heading into the village of **Hrašče**. As you pass through the village, look out for the storks' nests perched on the chimney tops. Just before reaching the main road again at the end of the village, turn →, again following the sign for cycle route 2. At the next T-junction, turn ← and then almost immediately → onto the dirt track. At the T-junction with the road, turn → (still following the route 2 sign). Follow this for around 2.5km, and then in the village of **Landol** turn ← at the crossroads, following the sign for *Šmihel* and the two cycle route signs (2 and 3). Follow this road past the dragon and, at the fire station, continue round to the **right** again, following the route 3 sign. This will bring you to a crossroads just below the church in **Šmihel**.

3 One of the arms of this crossroads is not a road at all but a track heading off to the →; take this, following the route 3 sign. This trail, following the signs all the way, leads through the woods and becomes a singletrack. It is one of the best sections on this route and it eventually leads out to the world-famous **Predjama Grad**. Follow, the little road up underneath the castle to the entrance, where you can pay to enter or have a bite to eat at the *gostilna* there. With your back to the castle, go ↑ through the car park. At the village of **Bukovje**, 1.5km from the castle, turn ← at the signs for routes 2 and 3 (which you now follow all the way to Studeno) and then turn → 100m later. After around 1.5km you'll come to the crossroads in **Belsko**; go ↑ and then, at the T-junction, turn ←. Follow this for just under a kilometre into the village of **Studeno**.

Speeding through the ancient forest on the way down to Pivka Jama

4 In Studeno, turn → opposite the small war memorial and then turn → at the fork next to the recycling bins. The road becomes a track again and you will pass under powerlines. About 200m after the lines, bear ← across the fields, heading towards the treeline. As you enter the trees, go ↑ and then ← at the next T-junction. About 500m later, look out for the **easy-to-miss** sign for *Pivka Jama* and turn →. At the T-junction with the road, turn ← and head through the **campsite** (don't worry about the barrier – you have access). If you have time, stop here to check out **Pivka Cave**. Follow the cycle route 2 signs right through the camp and back onto the track. Follow this now for 2.5km until you reach the T-junction with the road and turn →. Follow the road into **Postojna** and turn → next to the Epicenter Hotel, then turn immediately ← and follow this back to the car park.

Route 22

Lake Cerkno and the
caves of Rakov Škocja

22

START/FINISH	Jezerski Hram café, 500m south of Dolenje Jezero
DISTANCE	45.5km (28¼ miles)
ON ROAD	8.5km (5¼ miles)
OFF ROAD	37km (23 miles)
ASCENT	1190m (3905ft)
GRADE	▲
TIME	3–4hr 30min
MAP	Notranjski Kras, Brkini, Dolenjska, Bela Krajina
REFRESHMENTS	Hotel Rakov Škocjan (seasonal), Cerkno (all year)
PARKING	At the café
NOTE	The start point for this route should not be confused with the Jezerski Hram museum, which is in the village of Dolenje Jezero itself

OVERVIEW

This is a cracking route that begins on the shores of the mysterious, disappearing Lake Cerkno. Having spent a little time marvelling at this natural phenomenon, the route takes you off up into the wooded hills surrounding the lake and then, via a fabulous 8km descent, back down to the caves and karst features of the Rakov Škocjan park. Take a little time here to visit the main site – the Zelske Jame – before easing your way back to the beginning.

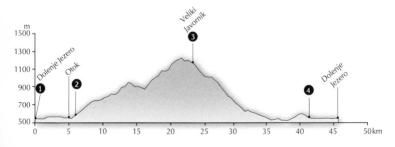

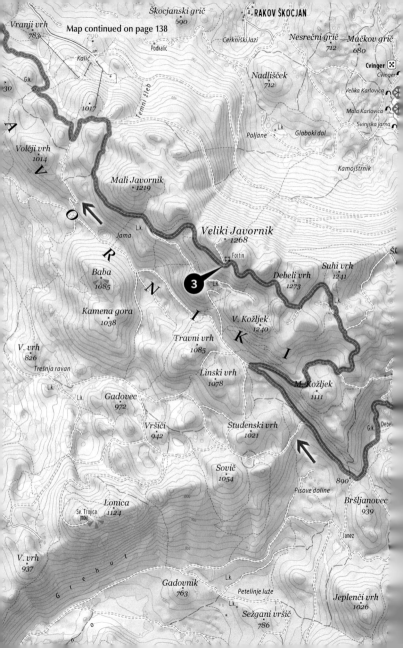

Map continued on page 138

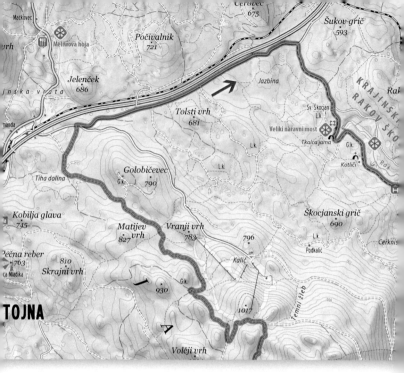

Directions

1 Turn ← out of the car park and head away from Dolenje Jezero. Very soon you are crossing either the lake or very flat, dry land, depending on the time of year. When you reach the gravel car park, turn ←, signposted for *Otok*. Some 4km later, at the T-junction just after **Otok**, turn ←, following the sign for *Laze*; this is the beginning of a long but steady 8km climb. Just under 1km later, turn → at the sign for *Otoška Dolina*.

2 Follow the trail steadily uphill now for a little less than 3km and then, at the fork, turn →, following the sign for *Cerknica 9*. At the three-way fork, take the ← branch uphill and then take the next major → about 1km later. Shortly after this, turn ← at the next T-junction. At the next fork, turn ←, heading downhill and following the signs for *Postojna, Pivka*. At the next T-junction, turn → (at the sign for *Postojna*) and then immediately → again at the WWII bunker. About 2km later, turn → back on yourself and uphill. This is the

Map continued on page 136

Enjoying the trails near Veliki Javornik

ROUTE 22 – LAKE CERKNO AND THE CAVES OF RAKOV ŠKOCJA 139

beginning of the final climb of the day. At the next fork, turn ← and continue uphill until the track flattens out and you come to the stone building at the foot of the peak **Veliki Javornik**. It is possible to take a small diversion on foot here to the summit for some great views north.

❸ After descending on the track for around 3km you'll come to a T-junction just after a small rise; turn ← and then, at the next fork about 600m further on, turn →, heading away from the sign for Postojna. Eventually (the descent from the summit is over 8km in total), this track will bring you down to a T-junction with a road. Turn → onto the road and continue along it for just under 3km. Turn →, following the sign for *Raka Škocjan*. This gravel road will take you all the way through to Zelše, but just after the Hotel Rakov Škocjan, about halfway, there is a place to pull off and head down into the gorge to explore the caves of the **Rakov Škocjan park**. Do take the time to do this, as they are well worthwhile.

❹ After the village of **Zelše**, turn → onto the road that skirts around the top of the industrial estate in the village of **Podskrajnik**. After around 2.5km, at the T-junction in **Dolenje Vas**, turn → and then ← over the bridge. This road then becomes a track, which first bends 90 degrees to the → and then to the ←. Follow the track to a crossroads in the village of **Dolenje Jezero** and turn →. Follow this road back to the car park.

At the bottom of the Škocjan caves

Route 23
Lake Cerknica circular

START/FINISH	Jezerski Hram café, 500m south of Dolenje Jezero
DISTANCE	24km (15 miles)
ON ROAD	11.5km (7¼ miles)
OFF ROAD	12.5km (7¾ miles)
ASCENT	380m (1245ft)
GRADE	■
TIME	1–2hr
MAP	Notranjski Kras, Brkini, Dolenjska, Bela Krajina
REFRESHMENTS	Cerknica town (all year)
PARKING	At the café
NOTE	The start point for this route should not be confused with the Jezerski Hram museum, which is in the village of Dolenje Jezero itself

55% OFF ROAD

OVERVIEW

Lake Cerknica is a fascinating phenomenon; it's an ephemeral lake, which essentially means that every year it simply disappears. What's actually happening is that, during the drier months, the waters head underground into the network of caverns below. This route is a very gentle but pleasant amble around the lake – or, depending on when you go, around the marshlands left once the lake has disappeared. The off-road sections could be tackled by something as simple as a hybrid bike so, if you're travelling with someone who isn't into the big mountains, this might be the route for them.

DIRECTIONS

1 Turn → out of the car park and follow the road (↑ at the crossroad in the village) all the way to **Cerknica** itself. At the T-junction with the main road, turn →.

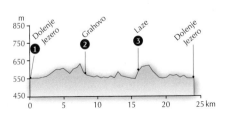

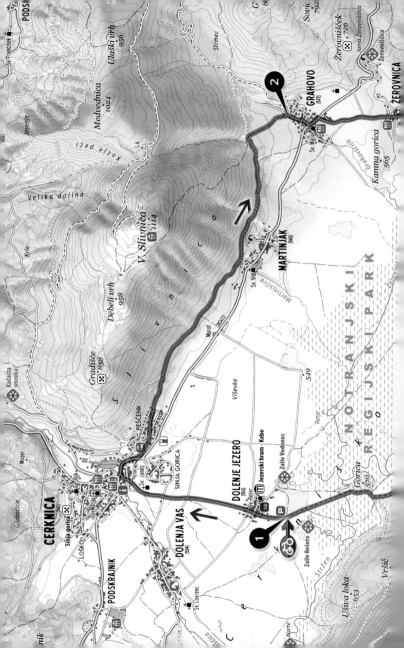

Riverside in the pretty village of Dolenje Jezero

About 300m later, take the ← heading uphill just before the large Mercator supermarket. At the crossroads, go ↑ onto the gravel track. Just over 2km later, at the fork above the next village (**Martinjak**), turn ← under the powerlines. Continue for almost another 2km, and at the crossroads next to the little shrine turn → and follow this track back down to the road at **Grahovo**.

A traditional Slovenian painted beehive

② At the T-junction with this road, turn ➔ towards the church that you can just see down the hill. When you reach the church, turn ⬅ at the crossroads and then almost immediately ➔, following signs for *Gor, Jezero* and *Žerovnica*. Continue on this road, going through the village of **Žerovnica**, for around 5.5km all the way to **Gornje Jezero**. In the village, turn ➔ next to the painted beehive, following signs for *Laze* and *Otok*. A little less than 2km later and after climbing up through the pretty village of **Laze**, turn ➔, back onto the track, at the T-junction with the sign for *Otok*.

③ After nearly 1.5km, at the next fork, take the ➔ (again, following the sign for *Otok*) and follow this track until it briefly becomes a road again in the village of **Otok**. Follow the road through the village and it again becomes a track; keep going along the western edge of the lake (with the best views) for around 3.5km until you reach a gravel parking area. Follow the track around to the ➔ and past the 'island' of **Gorica**. The road will start again and you simply follow this back to the **car park** at the beginning.

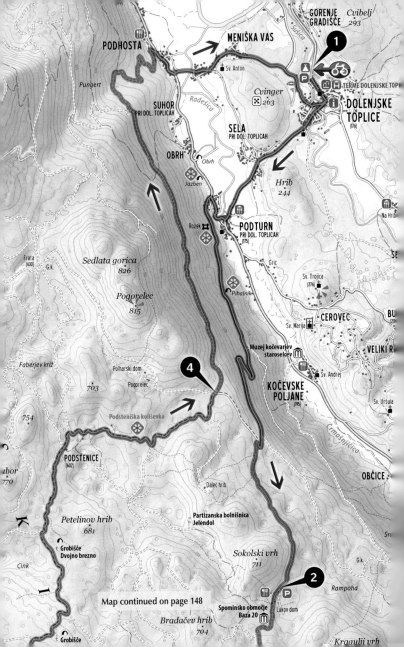

Map continued on page 148

Route 24

Dolenjske Toplice and the Partisans' forest

24

75% OFF ROAD

START/FINISH	Car park opposite the spa resort, Dolenjske Toplice
DISTANCE	41.5km (25¾ miles)
ON ROAD	11km (6¾ miles)
OFF ROAD	30.5km (19 miles)
ASCENT	1121m (3680ft)
GRADE	▲
TIME	2hr 30min–3hr 30min
MAP	Notranjski Kras, Brkini, Dolenjska, Bela Krajina
REFRESHMENTS	Dolenjske Toplice (take sandwiches)
PARKING	Large car park on northern edge of Dolenjske Toplice, on road from Novo Mesto

OVERVIEW

This route explores some of the forests of the Rog mountain range to the south-west of Dolenjske Toplice. The town itself is known for its spa, but the forests were part of the front line during World War II. The route will take you past the Baza 20 museum where the resistance command centre has been preserved, and it's definitely worth taking the time to explore the buildings, which remain in an excellent condition. The rest of the route meanders through the woods, giving you a great feeling for the remoteness of the terrain the Partisans held. Follow the IIIA bike signs all the way.

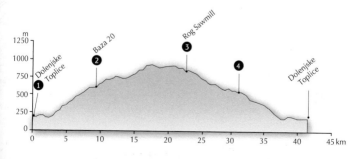

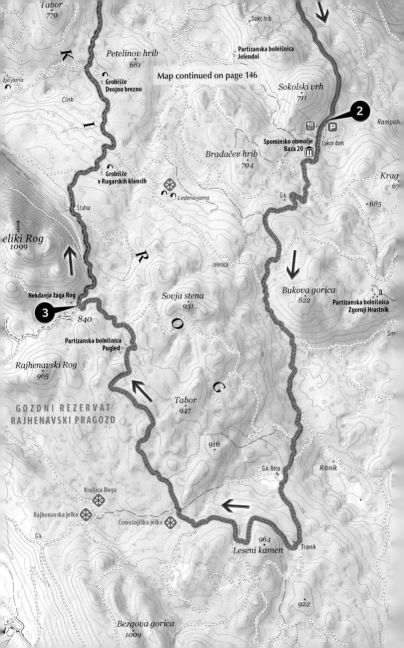

Tabor
770

Petelinov hrib
681

Dalec hrib

Partizanska bolnišnica
Jelendol

Sokolski vrh
711

Rampoh

Grobišče
Dvojno brezno

Map continued on page 146

Cink

Spominsko območje
Baza 20

2

Lukov dom

Krag
67

Grobišče
v Rugarskih klancih

Bradačev hrib
704

Štufna

G.k.

· 685

Ledena jama

eliki Rog
1099

Jelenica

R

Bukova gorica
822

Partizanska bolnišnica
Zgornji Hrastnik

Nekdanja žaga Rog

3   840

Sovja stena
931

Sm

Partizanska bolnišnica
Pugled

Rajhenavski Rog
965

Tabor
947

GOZDNI REZERVAT
RAJHENAVSKI PRAGOZD

916

G.k. Resa

Ribnik

Kraljica Roga

Rajhenavska jelka

Črmošnjiška jelka

Leseni kamen

964

Travnik

G.k.

922

Bezgova gorica
1009

DIRECTIONS

1 Turn ➜ out of the car park
and head through the
town on the main road.
After around 2.5km, at the
T-junction with the road at
Podturn, turn ➜, following
the blue bike sign for *IIIA*
and *IIIB*. A few hundred
metres later, turn ⬅,
following the sign for *Rog –
Baza 20*, and head uphill.
At the junction that follows
the two hairpin bends,
go ⬆, again following
the sign for *Baza 20*. This
will bring you up to the
museum of Baza 20 itself.
It's well worth a break here
to have a look around.

2 When you've had your fill
of history, keep on heading
uphill on the track and

*Make sure you know where you're going:
a typical junction in the woods just after Baza 20*

shortly you'll arrive at a fork; turn ⬅. Continue on for a couple of kilometres
until you reach a T-junction where you turn ➜, following the sign for *Mirna
Gora*. Then, at the next T-junction, turn ⬅ for *Mirna Gora* and *Travnik*. At the
next T-junction, turn ➜, following signs for *Resa* and *Mirna Gora*, and at the
next fork again turn ➜. A short while later, turn ⬅ at the fork following the
signs towards *Resa* and *Travnik*. Follow this track around the edge of the tiny
hamlet of **Resa**. The next fork comes just after the even smaller hamlet of
Travnik; turn ➜ here. At the next T-junction, turn ➜ again and then, a further
4km on, turn ⬅ at the next T-junction. This will bring you out to the clearing
at the **Rog**.

3 This spot is a nice place to eat a packed lunch and explore what's left of
the sawmill that supplied the Partisans in the forest. It was burnt down by
the Italians in 1942. Once you're ready to continue, turn ➜ onto the broad
gravel road and head downhill. About 2km further on there's the opportunity

Resa – one of the tiny hamlets hidden in the mountains

to take a diversion into the woods to look at the location of mass graves: alleged collaborators executed at the end of the war. Look out for the explanatory signs. At the next T-junction, follow the main track round to the ←, following signs for *Podturn* and *Baza 20* and continue on through the tiny hamlet of **Podstenice**. This will bring you to a crossroads where the paved road begins again.

4 Go ↑ here and prepare yourself for a lovely flowing descent. After about 4km of effortless downhill, turn → at the T-junction in **Podhosta**. Once you reach the ancient wagon by the side of the track, turn → back onto the road and then → again onto the main road. Take the next ← for *Dolenjske Toplice* and follow this road back to the outskirts of town. Turn ← at the T-junction and follow the road back through **Dolenjske Toplice** to the car park.

Route 25
Dolenjske Toplice and Soteska

25

START/FINISH	Car park opposite the spa resort, Dolenjske Toplice
DISTANCE	32km (19¾ miles)
ON ROAD	14km (8½ miles)
OFF ROAD	18km (11¼ miles)
ASCENT	830m (2725ft)
GRADE	■
TIME	2–3hr
MAP	Notranjski Kras, Brkini, Dolenjska, Bela Krajina
REFRESHMENTS	Dolenjske Toplice (take sandwiches)
PARKING	Large car park on northern edge of Dolenjske Toplice, on road from Novo Mesto

55% OFF ROAD

OVERVIEW

Beginning and ending in the thermal spa town of Dolenjske Toplice, this ride will take you up into the remote forested hills to the west of the town. There is a long, steady climb up through the pine forest that pays off with a lovely section of flowing downhill through a beech wood. You have less of the history of the previous route but it is also shorter. After your day out, feel free to treat yourself to a cake and a sauna or a soak at the spa. Follow the signs for IIIB all the way.

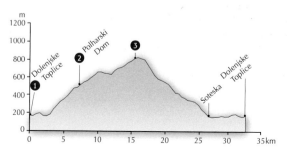

DIRECTIONS

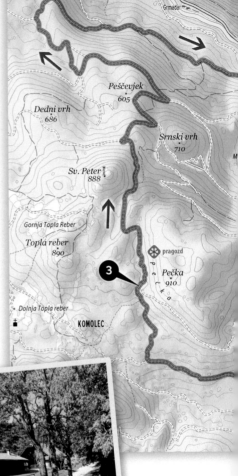

1 Turn → out of the car park and head through the town on the main road. After around 2.5km, at the T-junction with the road at **Podturn**, turn →, following the blue bike sign for *IIIA* and *IIIB*. A few hundred metres later, turn ←, following the sign for *Rog – Baza 20*, and head uphill. At the junction that follows the two hairpin bends, follow the road around to the →. At the crossroads at the end of the road section, go ↑. About a kilometre further on,

It's not open to the public, but Polharski Dom is a good spot for lunch

you'll come to the archery-hunting lodge called **Polharski Dom**. If it's not too early this is a good, open spot for lunch.

2 Turn → away from the buildings at the fork, shortly after which there is the possibility of a 20min walk up to the viewpoint on **Pogorelec**. Otherwise keep following the trail to the junction at the cottage 2.5km later, where you turn →, following sings for *Podhosta*. At the next fork, turn → and then ← immediately afterwards. Continue on to the next fork, where you turn →, and then on to the T-junction at which you turn ← and thus enter an area of ancient forest.

The unusual chapel at Soteska

3 Not long after this you'll finish the climbing and begin the long, glorious descent. At the first junction after you do, turn → and follow this down to a T-junction, where you turn ←. Turn ← again at the next T-junction and take the → at the next fork a little over 1km further on. At the next T-junction, turn → and enjoy a section of flowing downhill trail through the beech trees. At the next fork, after almost 4km of joyous riding, keep ← and continue downhill, coming out onto the road and turning ← to go over the bridge. Turn → at the T-junction after the bridge and continue past the chapel at **Soteska**. Some 2.5km after crossing the bridge, turn →, following the sign for *Dolenjske Toplice* and re-crossing the river. At the next T-junction turn ← and then ← again at the next T-junction. Follow the road back through **Dolenjske Toplice** to the car park.

Central and North East

Tackling the red descent from Bellevue summit station (Route 32)

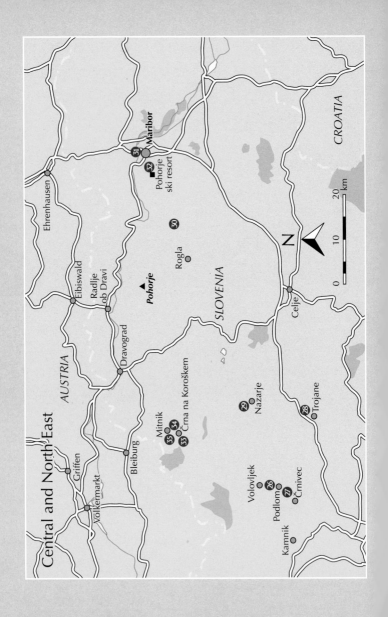

Approaching the plateau of Menina

I've cheated here a bit. This 'region' is in fact about half of the country and it covers almost everything east of Ljubljana. You won't find it listed on any official description of the country's regions, but it's useful for us as it gathers together rides from quite distant areas (as distant as you can get in Slovenia) that have a similar flavour. Away from some of the busier tourist areas, this region can provide you with mountains but with fewer other people and at less cost.

There are, of course, many towns and cities in this relatively large area, but for the purposes of this guide, the main ones we need to worry about are Maribor, Črna na Koroškem and Kamnik. Those craving a bit of civilisation (not to mention a Downhill World Cup venue) can head over to Maribor. Slovenia's second city, Maribor dates back to the medieval

period and still retains its old town core, although many of its grander buildings date from the time of the Hapsburgs. The area surrounding Maribor is famous for its vineyards and, indeed, the world's oldest cropping vine can be found in the town centre. West of there, virtually on the Austrian border, is Črna na Koroškem – rightly famed for its beautiful countryside. The town itself is quite small but the mountains that cluster around it provide ample opportunity for biking (and other sports), and Slovenia's first bike park was established here. Finally, a little further west still, lies Kamnik: a quaint little medieval town just a short drive north of Ljubljana. Legend has it that the town is presided over by the Countess Veronika – a half-snake, half-woman who guards the treasure of Mali Grad (the little castle).

Accommodation

There are plenty of options for accommodation in Maribor. For those looking for high-end, you could do worse than Hotel Habakuk (www.hotel-habakuk.si/en). Right at the foot of the Downhill park, this wellness hotel provides information about activities (including biking) in the area as well as offering excellent facilities. For those on a budget, The Hostel Uni (www.youth-hostel.si, go to 'hostels' and then search Maribor under 'choose city') offers private rooms right in the centre of town with free wi-fi and information about the locality. Between those two extremes is Hotel Bellevue (www.hotelbellevue.si/en). Surprisingly good value, this hotel, located on the top of the hill overlooking Maribor and at the top of the bike park, has spectacular views. It also has bike hire facilities.

There's not a great deal of accommodation actually in the town of Črna na Koroškem, but as there are skiing areas in the vicinity, there are plenty of other places to stay nearby. One such is Golte (www.golte.si/eng), a mid-range hotel. It's a bit remote at the top of the ski runs but it's worth the effort with some fabulous facilities. The Ecohotel Koroš (www.bikenomad.com) is a bit more budget than Golte and is probably the best option for most, however. It is a specialist bike hotel with superb facilities and even has a trail in its grounds.

Finally, Kamnik provides all the charm of a medieval town and its accommodation reflects this. Most accommodation in town is found in traditional houses such as Pri Cesarju (pricesarju.si/en), a 19th-century inn. However, just outside town can be found an excellent thermal resort called Snovik (terme-snovik.si/en), which includes a lovely waterpark for cooling off after a ride on those hot summer days. In addition, Kamp Reznik provides excellent camping facilities for both camper vans and tents alike (kampresnik.com).

Services

Absolutely the best place to hire bikes in this region is at the Ecohotel Koroš, mentioned above. They are passionate about biking and keep a range of bikes available. However, if you're not heading that far north, perfectly acceptable bikes can be rented from Rent-a-bike Slovenia (www.rentabike.si) in Ljubljana. In Maribor, head over to the bike park and you can rent either a downhill bike or a Specialized cross-country model (www.bikeparkpohorje.si/en)

Once again, the tourist information centres in Kamnik, Trbovlje, Črna na Koroškem, Ravne na Koroškem and Maribor all have very useful information and specially printed biking maps.

Emergencies

There are good health centres and clinics as well as pharmacies in all of the following towns: Ravne na Koroškem, Trbovlje and Maribor.

Route 26
Velika Planina

START/FINISH	Gostilna Zmai (inn), Volovljek
DISTANCE	18km (11 miles)
ON ROAD	0km
OFF ROAD	18km (11 miles)
ASCENT	780m (2560ft)
GRADE	▲
TIME	2–2hr 30min
MAP	Alpski Svet – Vzhodni Del
REFRESHMENTS	Zeleni Rob (every day in season; Friday, Saturday and Sunday off-season)
PARKING	Layby at Volovljek on road between Podlom and Luče, opposite Gostilna Zmai inn at head of pass

OVERVIEW

Visiting Velika Planina (The Big Meadow) is something of a tradition for Slovenes. High in the mountains is a summer meadow dotted about with quaint, traditional huts and it's a natural tourist magnet for those seeking fresh, alpine air. It is possible to stay in the huts but most head up there for the day, either hiking, skiing or, of course, biking. This route is brief and non-technical and the climb is surprisingly short (given the ultimate altitude reached), but it's still not a route to be trifled with and the weather on the top can be very different from even the elevated starting point. However, the rewards are worth it: it's an absolute must-do.

DIRECTIONS

① From the layby, cross the road and take the track to the → of the *gostilna* (restaurant), following the sign for *Velika Planina*. Your climb begins straight away. At the fork about 1.5km further on, turn → (there is parking here if you

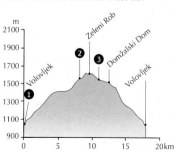

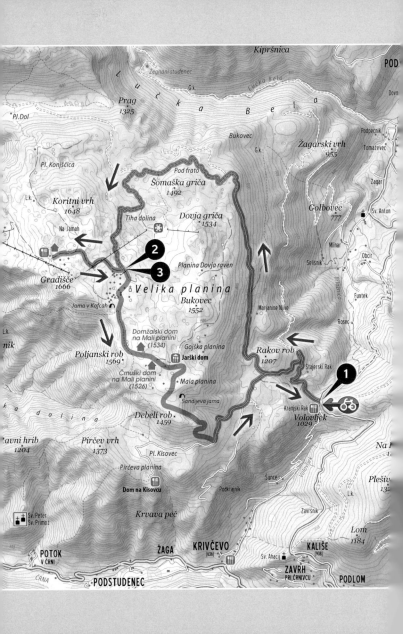

The quaint alpine village of Velika Planina

wish to miss out some of the climbing). Follow this trail steadily uphill for another 5km, and then at the fork turn ←, following signs for *Zeleni Rob* and *Veliki Stan*. After 2km this trail will bring you to a car park and then, passing under a ski lift, you'll come out onto the plateau of **Velika Planina**.

2 At the first few huts turn →, following the sign for *Šimnovec*. This section, 2.5km there and back, can be missed out but it does bring you to an excellent lunch stop and a fabulous view. At the next T-junction, turn → and follow this trail all the way to Zeleni Rob, the little restaurant at the top of the ski lift out of the valley. Take a well-earned rest, admire the view and contemplate the downhill mountain biking that is possible from here straight down to the valley. After lunch, return the way you came as far as the first set of huts on the plateau.

3 Turn →, following the sign for *Mala Planina*. Follow the main track around to the **right** and into the main part of the village that sprawls around the plateau, turning ← just before it goes up hill, passing the church and pond on the **left**. At the fork in the middle of the field, turn ← and head past **Domžalski Dom** (where it's also possible to get food). At the crossroads

Alpine scenery at Jarški Dom

just after Domžalski Dom, go ↑, following the sign for *Jarški Dom*. At the fork just after the S-bends at **Jarški Dom**, turn →. Follow this trail across the plateau and then downhill, and at the next T-junction turn ← over the cattle grid. This track runs for around 1.5km downhill to the next T-junction where you turn →, back onto your ascent from the beginning. Follow this back down to the car park at **Volovljek**.

Route 27
Menina Planina

START/FINISH	Gostišče GTC (inn), Črnivec
DISTANCE	38.5km (24 miles)
ON ROAD	3.5km (2¼ miles)
OFF ROAD	35km (21¾ miles)
ASCENT	1340m (4395ft)
GRADE	▲
TIME	3–4hr
MAP	Alpski Svet – Vzhodni Del
REFRESHMENTS	Dom na Menini (every day in season; Saturdays and Sundays out of season)
PARKING	At the inn

OVERVIEW

Menina Planina is not as popular as its more illustrious neighbour Velika Planina, visited in the previous route. However, it has a similar landscape, and because of its Cinderella status it is always much quieter than its famous cousin. The route winds up through wooded slopes until you reach the alpine pasture and the mountain refuge which serves food and, should you need it, has accommodation.

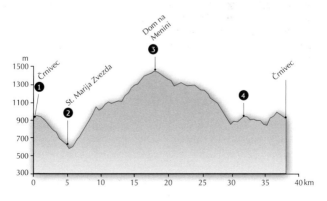

After that, you cross the plateau and begin an extended but gentle descent back through the woods to your starting point.

Directions

1 Out of the car park, turn ← onto the main road and then immediately ← again down the side of the inn. After a short time, turn ← at the sign for *Toman* and then, at the next fork, turn ←, again following the sign for *Toman*. Follow this track past Kmetija Toman (shown on the map as **Toman**) and then, at the T-junction, turn ←, following this track until you reach the

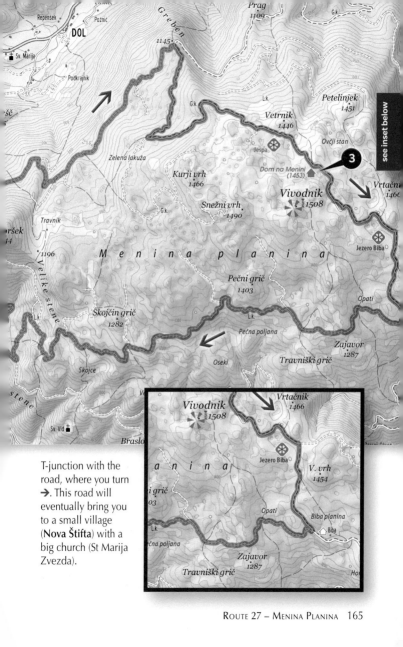

see inset below

T-junction with the road, where you turn →. This road will eventually bring you to a small village (**Nova Štifta**) with a big church (St Marija Zvezda).

2 Follow the road around to the **right** and then, just after the village, turn onto the track on the →, following the sign for *Menina 14km*. Your climb begins here. Go ↑ at the next junction about 0.5km further on. For the next section, keep following signs for *Menina*. After another 3km, turn ← at the fork and ← again at the next fork. At the next T-junction turn →, and then ← at the next fork. This will, eventually, bring you out onto the plateau and up to the refuge **Dom na Menini** at 1453m. Take time for a break and a spot of lunch. If you have the legs, you can take the walk from here to the summit of **Vivodnik** for some spectacular views.

Nova Štifta: A Little village with a big church

3 When you're ready to continue, keep on the track past the refuge. At the next fork, turn → and head past *Lake Biba* – a limestone sinkhole. At the T-junction after around 1.4km, turn → back into the woods. Keep on the main trail now for about 6km until you come to a **right-hand** hairpin bend; follow the trail around and then turn ← about 300m later. This turning is just before a **left-hand** hairpin at the sign for *Partizanska Bolnica*. **Make sure you make this turn, as continuing on will bring you down into the wrong valley.**

4 A further 2km along the track, turn → at the sign for *Sv. Prevala* and continue ↑ through all the junctions for the next 3.3km until you reach the T-junction with the road. Turn → and head through the village of **Poljana** and back onto the dirt track. Head up and then down, turning ← when you reach the track that was your ascent. Head back down to the car park at **Črnivec**.

Route 28
Jesenovo and Krvavica

28

START/FINISH	Gostišče Trojane (service station), Trojane
DISTANCE	25.5km (15¾ miles)
ON ROAD	15km (9¼ miles)
OFF ROAD	10.5km (6½ miles)
ASCENT	1025m (3360ft)
GRADE	■
TIME	1hr 30min–2hr 30min
MAP	Alpski Svet – Vzhodni Del
REFRESHMENTS	Zajčeva Koča (weekends in season), Trojane
PARKING	At the service station

40% OFF ROAD

OVERVIEW

The Slovenian for black pudding is *krvavica*, and this route, while not necessarily including any of the savoury pig produce, does take in a peculiar hill of the same name. There is quite a bit of road to this route (some of which can be taken out by starting and finishing at Šentgotard). To make up for that, there are some very attractive views and that unusually named hill with great views from the top. While there's a lot of ascent for a short route, there are no long climbs as there are in some of the more mountainous parts.

DIRECTIONS

1 Beginning in the giant car park at the service station in Trojane – a hangover from the days before the highway when this was a stopping point on the main route from Ljubljana to Maribor – turn ➔ and then ➔ again at the sign for *Zagorje* and *Izlake*. At the end of the small village, turn ←, following the sign for *Šentgotard*. After the village of **Šentgotard**, turn ➔, following the sign for *Čemšenik*. After around 4km and passing through **Brezje** and **Dobrljevo**, this road will bring you to the church of Marije Vnezbovzete in **Čemšenik** itself, where you turn ← then ➔ at the tree with a heart on it. Follow this for just over a kilometre until you reach the tiny cable car winch hut.

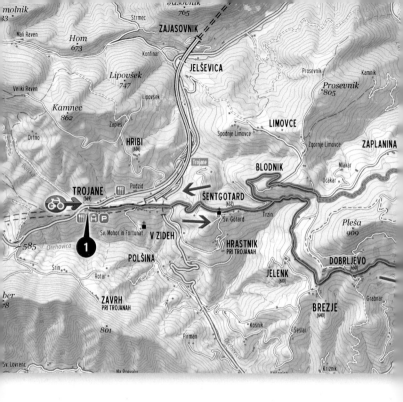

2 Turn ← at the hut to pass underneath the cables and follow the track for just over a kilometre into the village of **Jessenovo**, where you turn ← (there is a sign for *Znojile* facing away from you). Follow this for about another 3km before turning ← uphill at the little hut called Počivališče Pod Babo on

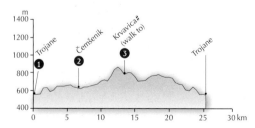

the outskirts of **Znojile**. This short section is the toughest climb on the route up to the farm as you leave the trees. Turn → here at the sign for *Zajčeva Koča*. Follow the trail over the open land to the tree line and turn ← into the trees at the sign for *Krvavica*. Enjoy this short but lovely downhill section. When you reach the T-junction at the bottom, take the time to

The church of St Mary (Marije Vnezbovzete) in Čemšenik

Enjoying the downhill to 'Mount Black Pudding'

park the bike up and make the 20-minute walk to the summit of **Krvavica**. (Turning → would take you to Zajčeva Koča for lunch.)

❸ Having enjoyed the views from the top of Krvavica, return to the trail and, imagining we've just come down the little bit of singletrack from the previous section, turn ← (or right if you've got your back to Krvavica). After 1km, at the next T-junction, turn ← and then ← at the fork as you leave the trees (follow the sign for *Čemšeniška*). This trail will continue now for around 5km until you reach a T-junction with the road. Turn → onto the road and then immediately ←. At the next T-junction turn ←, then turn → at the next T-junction, signed for *Šentgotard*. Follow your outward route back to the car park at **Trojane**.

Route 29
The churches of Čreta

29

Start/Finish	Grad Vrbovec (castle), Nazarje
Distance	27km (16¾ miles)
On road	13km (8 miles)
Off road	14km (8¾ miles)
Ascent	1370m (4495ft)
Grade	■
Time	2hr 30min–3hr 30min
Map	Alpski Svet – Vzhodni Del
Refreshments	Dom na Čreta (all year, weekends and public holidays)
Parking	Car park next to castle

Overview

This route is a quiet delight. You may see walkers out on your journey but the chances of seeing other bikers are slim as this is a forgotten little treat. Taking a tough climb out of Nazarje, you'll reach the ridge above Čreta before contouring round (with just a bit more climbing) above the valley floor. The two churches on the route are popular spots to visit on foot for the locals, but you'll cover considerably more distance and finish with an extended descent back to the flood plain.

Directions

① Turn ← out of the car park onto the main road and then ← again, following the signs for *Čreta* (which you follow all the way to Čreta itself) and the *Tuš*. Cross the bridge, then

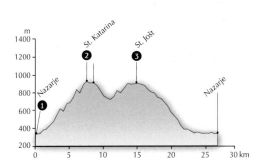

Commemorating the fallen Partisans

turn → and go ↑ at the crossroads 600m from the start (don't follow the road round to the right). After two hairpins, go ↑ at the next junction and then turn → at the following fork about 400m further on. Continue on this main route now for another 4km or so through **Lomšek** and **Rebernik**. At the next junction, go ↑ (still following signs) and follow the road and then the trail up to the next T-junction. Turn → (following the sign for *Vransko*) and after around 600m this will bring you up onto the open plateau. Here (at the wooden memorial to the Partisans),

Riding past the church of St Jošt

you have the opportunity to take the trail to the **left** down to **Dom na Čreti** (signposted Koča na Čreti) for some refreshment.

2 Once refreshed and returned to the trail, continue to the T-junction just after the first of the churches – **St Katarina** – and turn **←**. At the next T-junction turn **→**, following signs for *Vransko*, *Tolsti Vrh* and *Lipa*. About 3km further on, at the apex of a **left-hand** hairpin, turn **→** at the sign for *Jeronim* and *Sv. Jošt*. At the next fork, turn **→** uphill and then **←** at the next junction, following a sign for *Sv. Jošt*. At the next fork turn **←** and, after just over a kilometre, this will bring you to the second of the two churches – **St Jošt** – precariously perched on the side of the valley.

3 After the church and after you've begun your descent, at the next T-junction turn **←** and follow this trail all the way down to the road. After around 5.5km, turn **→** at the T-junction with the road and then take the next **←**, doubling back on yourself and turning **→** immediately towards **Potok**. About 1km further, once on the flat valley bottom, turn **→** over the tiny bridge. In the village of **Kokarje**, at the crossroads, turn **←** then take your second **→** (just after the entrance to the farmyard). At the fork 200m further on, turn **←** onto the gravel track and then continue for just over 1.5km until you reach the next T-junction. Here, turn **→** and then immediately **←** and follow this road along the flat back to **Vrbovec Castle** – in which there happens to be a very good restaurant.

Route 30

The nature reserve of Pohorje

START/FINISH	Car park north of Matevžev Vrh
DISTANCE	30km (18½ miles)
ON ROAD	0km
OFF ROAD	30km (18½ miles)
ASCENT	680m (2230ft)
GRADE	■
TIME	2–3hr
MAP	Štajerska
REFRESHMENTS	Dom na Osankarici (all year), Koča na Klopnem vrhu (1.2km off route; in season)
PARKING	Note that the car park is quite remote and requires reasonable navigation just to find it. Head out of Maribor via Spodnje Hoče to the Russian Cottage at Areh. Roughly 5km further, look out for the RH turn down towards the car park.

OVERVIEW

If you're looking for a gentle bike through the woods then you could do far worse than this ride. Its whole length is off-road (although cars do still occasion- ally appear) and is entirely within the Pohorje nature

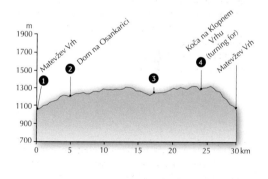

reserve – a giant area of ancient woodland. There is a possible excursion to the famous Black Lake, and to finish there is a genuinely delightful, easy singletrack downhill back to the car park. You may also glimpse wild boar. For a relaxing rest day or a family excursion, this is hard to beat.

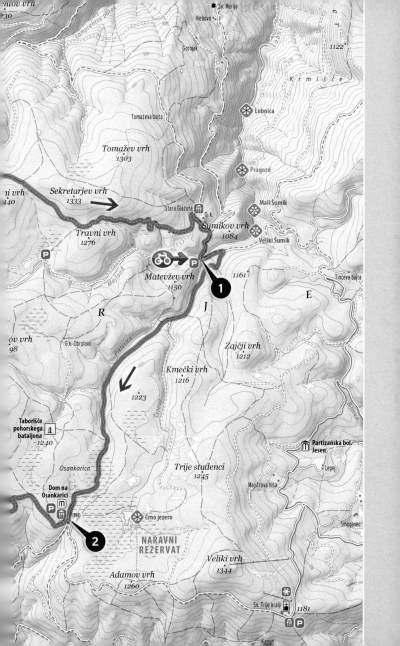

DIRECTIONS

1 From the car park take the track north-east uphill, back towards Areh, and turn ➔ after about 300m at the sign for *Osankarica 6*. Continue on this trail for about 3km before turning ⬅ at the next fork, again at a sign for *Osankarica*. Once you get to the car park, turn ➔ at the fork towards the restaurant. This is **Dom na Osankarici**. Although it's early on in the ride, it's possible to take a break here and it's also the starting point for the stroll to **Črno Jezero** (or Black Lake) – a natural feature worth the 20-minute walk.

2 Having visited the lake and refreshed yourself at the *gostilna*, continue, following the *2:1* cycle route signs. At the crossroads further on, go ⬆. You now follow this trail for another 6km or so before coming to a blockage in the track; go around this (still following the *2:1* signs) and continue on (under a barrier) to the next T-junction, where you turn ➔.

3 Believe it or not, this gravel track is now a road. You'll see few cars, but **take care** for the next couple of kilometres. Turn ➔ at the sign for *Občina Lovrenc Na Pohorju*. At the next junction, some 5km later, it is possible to take a short (1.2km) diversion **left** to the **Koča na Klopnem vrhu** for some

The famous Črno Jezero or Black Lake

Enjoying the stretch of singletrack after the short, sharp climb

refreshment, in season. Otherwise, turn → and then immediately take the →
fork at the sign for *Šumik*. There is a very short, **very technical climb** just here
but it is over quickly and bikes can be pushed if necessary.

4 After the short, sharp shock of the climb, enjoy the non-technical singletrack
that follows. After about 2km, at the next fork, turn ←, following signs for
Bajgat and *Ruška Koča*. Just after a hut on the **right-hand** side, turn ← at the
T-junction and follow the trail down to the next T-junction at **Stara Glažuta**
where you turn →. There is one final T-junction where you turn → again and
this will bring you back to the car park near **Matevžev Vrh**.

Following the well-marked trails towards Brestrnica

Route 31
Maribor and its surroundings

START/FINISH	Old town square, Maribor
DISTANCE	26.5km (16½ miles)
ON ROAD	17.5km (11 miles)
OFF ROAD	9km (5½ miles)
ASCENT	840m (2755ft)
GRADE	■
TIME	2–2hr 30min
MAP	Štajerska
REFRESHMENTS	Maribor (take sandwiches)
PARKING	Plenty of options in Maribor

OVERVIEW

Maribor, Slovenia's second city, is a beautiful old town, much of which remains from the time of the Hapsburgs. Its surroundings are equally attractive and this route, beginning in

the medieval town centre, wends its way out into the countryside immediately surrounding the city. It passes through vineyards and forests and includes a spectacular view back to the town from the high point of the ride at the church of St Urban. There is a lot of road on this route and the off-road is non-technical, but there is still much to commend it.

DIRECTIONS

❶ Facing the entrance to the museum, keep it on your left and head **north**, keeping ↑ over three junctions until you reach the park. Keep ↑ through the park until you reach a fountain 1km from the start of the route, where you join the road over to your right-hand side, turning ← onto the road.

After another 1.3km, at the top of the steep climb, turn → at the *3:1* cycle sign. At the next fork 1km further on, turn ← (following the bee sign) and then, at the T-junction, turn →. This will bring you out of the woods a kilometre later onto a ridge above vineyards and to a hunting high-seat.

2 Just after the high-seat, the trail hairpins around to the right; turn ← off the apex of this bend and then follow the trail around to the →. This will bring you onto a lovely section of downhill singletrack. Just under a kilometre later, at the next junction, turn ←, following the *3:1* sign. This brings you to a T-junction with a major road; **exercise caution** as you turn ← here. Turn → at the sign for *Sv. Urban* and begin the tough-ish climb through the village of **Bračko** with its rustic road-side art. At the next fork, keep ←, following the *3:1* sign again. This will bring you to the fork for the road up to the church of St Urban. Our route heads → here, but it's worth the extra little effort to go to the **church** for the spectacular views over the surrounding countryside.

3 After taking the → just below the church, turn → off the road about 2km later onto the gravel track at the *3:1* sign. Follow the track down to the T-junction with the road and turn ←, this time following the sign

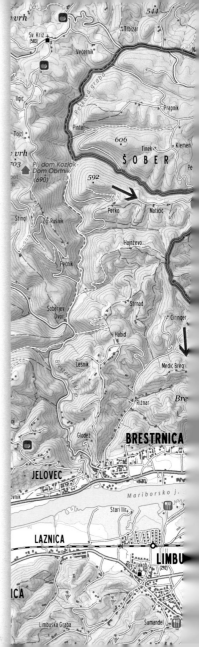

The fountain in Maribor's central park

for *3:2*. At the fork, turn **←** for *Brestrnica*. Around 2km later, take the **easy-to-miss ←** over the bridge at the sign for *Kamnica*. At the T-junction with the road around 2km later, turn **→** and then immediately **→** again (sign *3:1*), and at the next T-junction turn **←**, following the signs for *Prevolšek* and *3:1*. At the next fork, turn **←**, passing the sign for *Medič* on the right.

❹ When you reach the T-junction at the bridge, turn **→** and follow the road into **Kamnica**. Go **↑** at the crossroads and then **←** at the next T-junction. Turn **→** at the next T-junction, signposted for the *Hipodrom Kamnica*. As you enter **Maribor** on this road, bear round to the **←** next to the Mercator supermarket and follow this back to the centre.

Route 32

The Maribor downhill park

START/FINISH	Bottom Pohorje cable car station, south-west of Maribor
DISTANCE	15.5km (9½ miles)
ON ROAD	1.5km (1 mile)
OFF ROAD	14km (8½ miles)
ASCENT	950m (3115ft)
GRADE	■/▲/◆
TIME	1–2hr
MAP	Štajerska
REFRESHMENTS	Upper cable car station (all year)
PARKING	Car park at lower cable car station

OVERVIEW

Maribor is known for its skiing and hosts a leg of the world cup. However, in the late spring and summer its slopes are converted for use by mountain bikers and there are a choice of routes (and grades) from the top back down. It is, of course, possible to take your bike on the cable car up to the top station – which is particularly useful if you have a heavy downhill bike. For the rest of us though, there's a pleasant climb up through the woods on the back of the hill, which makes the fun at the end of the ride all the more rewarding.

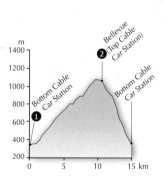

DIRECTIONS

① Head to the back of the car park and take a ➔ into the woods. When you meet the road after about 300m, go ↑. At the next T-junction turn ← at the sign for *0:1*. This road quickly becomes a gravel track and you begin the

ascent. After almost 2.5km, at the next fork, turn ← again, following the *0:1* sign. Keep going until you reach the summit of **Pohorje** and the hotel Bellevue.

2 The track eventually brings you out at the top cable car station. Here there is refreshment and information about the route options for the downhill. Off the top, there are two main options – a blue and a red – but these split at various points and give you further options for making it harder (up to black runs) or easier. They all bring you back down to the bottom cable car station and your car park. Take your pick and enjoy.

Route 33

The Najevnik Linden Tree

33

START/FINISH	Central roundabout, Črna na Koroškem
DISTANCE	17.5km (11 miles)
ON ROAD	6.5km (4 miles)
OFF ROAD	11km (7 miles)
ASCENT	1045m (3430ft)
GRADE	■
TIME	1–2hr
MAP	Alpski Svet – Vzhodni Del
REFRESHMENTS	Črna na Koroškem
PARKING	Plenty of spaces in Črna na Koroškem but the car parks are small and spread around town

65%
OFF ROAD

OVERVIEW

Črna na Koroškem is famous for two things: its mining history and the Najevnik Linden Tree. The linden has a long history of significance in Slovenian culture as the centre of a village and the place where the elders would gather. The Najevnik Linden is not only the oldest of its kind in Slovenia (over 700 years) but it's also the place that the founders of the Republic of Slovenia gathered

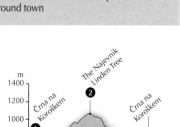

just a month after declaring independence from Yugoslavia. This short but sweet route will take you up into the foothills of the mountains to deposit you at this place of pilgrimage for Slovenians.

DIRECTIONS

① Head south-east out of town on the Šoštanj road. After about 3km, turn ➔ at the sign for *Ludranski Vrh*. This road becomes a track and then a reasonably steep climb. At the T-junction after the climb, turn ➔. At the sign for *Vesevk*, follow the hairpin to the ⬅. At the T-junction turn ➔, following the sign for

Lipa. This will bring you to the tree (**Najevska lipa**) itself.

❷ After admiring the linden, continue round to the ← on the track. At the next T-junction turn →, away from Gotec. At the next fork another kilometre further on, bear ← downhill. This will start you off on an exceptional, long stretch of easy downhill. When it finally finishes at the T-junction with the road, turn ← and follow the road back into **Črna na Koroškem**.

The 700-year-old Najevnik Linden Tree

Route 34

The three valleys route

34

Start/Finish	Central roundabout, Črna na Koroškem
Distance	39.5km (24½ miles)
On road	17.5km (11 miles)
Off road	22km (13½ miles)
Ascent	1925m (6315ft)
Grade	▲
Time	4–5hr
Map	Alpski Svet – Vzhodni Del
Refreshments	Črna na Koroškem (take sandwiches)
Parking	Plenty of spaces in Črna na Koroškem but the car parks are small and spread around town

55% OFF ROAD

Overview

A longer and harder route than Route 33, with a good deal of climbing, this ride takes in three of the prettiest valleys in the Črna region. First you make your way up the gentle Bistra. Then you drop down via the dramatic church of St Jacob and head up the Koprivna all the way to the Austrian border before dropping down, through the Krajinski Park Topla (the Topla Landscape Park), to the Meža valley and from there home. On the way you'll get a real feel of this remote, mountainous land, from its rolling alpine pastures to its hard climbs and long descents.

Directions

1 Head west out of town on the Koprivna road and turn ← just before the first bridge. After the stadium, at the fork, bear ← and then, at the end of the village, go ↑ over the bridge and onto the track to the ← on the other side. Follow this to the road and turn ←.

A wildflower meadow in the Bistra valley

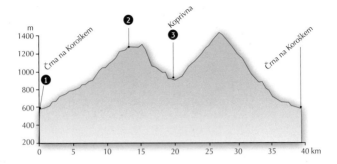

After about 2.5km turn → at the sign for *Turistična Kmetija Plaznik*; this takes you into the first of the three valleys – the Bistra. The road becomes a track and you stay on the main trail for around 5.5km until you reach a fork at the sign for *Ratih*, where you bear ←. At the next T-junction turn →, following the main trail and the yellow trail markers. This will bring you out to another T-junction with a more substantial dirt road. Go ↑ onto the little level area where you'll see that it's actually a crossroads.

② At the crossroads, turn → down the trail indicated by the small red sign for *Olševa*. After a couple of kilometres you'll come to two **right-hand** turns close together; turn → down the first one (the other is marked Olševa). This becomes an interesting descent through the forest. Keep ↑ until you approach the church of **St Jacob** and you reach a T-junction. Turn ← here (turning right would take you to the church itself). After a short descent, turn → at the next T-junction away from the house and then → again at the next T-junction. This will bring you down to the little settlement of **Lipold** at the bottom of the Koprivna valley, and a T-junction with a large yellow farmhouse in front of you and a small shelter to your left.

③ At this T-junction, turn ← up the valley. Continue ahead after the road becomes a track for around 3km, going through **Brodnik** and passing the turn off for Zdovc, and then turn → at the signs for *Topla, Šopart, Ledrovec*. This is the border with Austria; if you look in the stream by the track you'll see a border post. Follow the trail for around 6km, going up and then, after passing over the saddle, down again. At the fork near the house, bear ← towards the house and then turn → at the road (which begins a few metres to the left). Follow this road for nearly 5.5km all the way down to the T-junction with the bigger road opposite the log cabin. Turn ← and follow this road all the way back into **Črna**.

Descending towards the church of St Jacob

Descending through a meadow near Rišperg

Route 35

Peca

START/FINISH	Restaurant Okrepčevalnica Matjaž, Mitnik
DISTANCE	16.5km (10¼ miles)
ON ROAD	1.5km (1 mile)
OFF ROAD	15km (9¼ miles)
ASCENT	835m (2740ft)
GRADE	■
TIME	2–2hr 30min
MAP	Alpski Svet – Vzhodni Del
REFRESHMENTS	Koča na Pikovem (all year, closed Mondays)
PARKING	Take the Koprivna road out of Črna and take the first right. Follow signs to Mitnik. Park in the restaurant car park.

90% OFF ROAD

OVERVIEW

The final route in this book is a gentle ride around the beautiful mountains of Koroška. It begins and ends in the tiny settlement of Mitnik where in winter they hold a snow-castle building competition. The route takes you, via forest tracks and through alpine meadows, to a charming mountain restaurant and then back down again. It's not technical, there's only a bit of climbing and it's a lovely half-day out with a bite to eat on the way (and maybe a drink).

DIRECTIONS

① Ride back the way you drove in for 150m and then turn ➔ back on yourself and uphill. Follow the sign for *Štopar*. A short way further on, turn ← away from **Najbrž**. There is a short section of road not long after this; shortly after it finishes, about 1.2km from your last junction, turn ➔ at

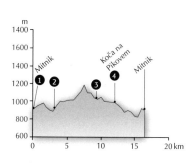

the T-junction (follow signs for *Mihev* and *Žačen*). At the next crossroads, around 400m further on, continue ↑, following the sign for *Dom na Peci*.

2 Keep following this trail for around 3km until you turn ←, again following signs towards *Dom na Peci*. Shortly after this, turn → at the sign for *Rišperg* and tackle the stiff-ish climb. After you reach the top, take the → fork and then go ↑ onto the singletrack across the fields. At this point you're passing along the Austrian border. After re-entering the woods, at the next T-junction turn → (downhill) and then you'll come to a five-way crossroads. Keep ↑, past the memorial and bear slightly ← uphill. Now keep an eye out for the **difficult-to-spot→**, signposted for *Pikovo*, which is the beginning of the singletrack.

3 The difficult start to this singletrack eases as you progress. About 500m later, at the crossroads, turn → for *Pikovo* and then, at the next T-junction, turn ←, following the red-and-white roundels. After a slight rise, take the → fork and then, at the T-junction, turn → to again follow the sign for *Pikovo*. Follow this trail down to the church and the restaurant **Koča na Pikovem**. Take a rest and try the food, or if you're feeling fresh, carry on.

4 To continue, turn ← at the church (if you've just come down the trail). At the next T-junction, 300m later, turn → and then take your second → towards Petek (off the middle of a **right-hand** hairpin bend) about a kilometre later. After a slight rise, bear ← and, at the next T-junction, turn → downhill, following the sign for *Helena*. At the T-junction with the road, turn → and then turn → again at the following T-junction, signposted for *Mitnik*. Follow this back to the car park at **Mitnik**.

Time to eat at Koča na Pikovem

Appendix A
Slovenian language

Slovenia is a small country with a tiny population; nobody bothers to learn their language. As a consequence, and because tourism is one of their major industries, everyone you're likely to meet will speak excellent English. A standard response to the question, 'Do you speak English?' is, 'A little,' followed by a near-fluent conversation.

That said, it is always useful – not to mention polite – to learn a bit of the language of the country you're visiting. As Slovenia has the decency to provide us with some truly beautiful bike rides and some of the cheapest nights out in Europe, it's the least we can do. Here, then, is a handy glossary, but first…

Some notes on pronunciation
Slovenian is a Slavic language coming from the same root as Russian, Polish or Czech, and at first sight it can appear daunting with its accented letters and alien words. But just as Slovenian also contains words with Latin roots to make us feel more at home, it is also surprisingly easy to learn to pronounce.

Without exception, letters and words are pronounced consistently, so once you have learned how to do it properly, it's always the same.

As a general rule, letters in Slovenian are pronounced in the same way they are in English, with these notable exceptions:

Letter	Pronounced
C	'ts' as in hats
Č	'ch' as in church
G	hard g as in goat
H	'ch' as in loch (we have no real equivalent in English but the Scots come closest; it's a sort of half-growl at the back of the throat)
I	'ee' as in seen

Letter	Pronounced
J	'y' as in yellow
Š	'sh' as in shutter
V	'f' as in four
W	'v' as in victor
Ž	'j' as in Jack (again, we have no real equivalent in English; it's actually closer to the French j as in Jacques)
AV	'ow' as in ow

All letters are pronounced, so an e at the end of a word has a sound: for example, the word *limonade* is pronounced 'lee-mo-na-deh'. Finally, it's usually the penultimate syllable that is stressed, but if you're getting that technical you're probably already learning Slovenian.

Useful words

Greetings

English	Slovenian	Pronounced
hello	*dober dan*	'dobber dan'
hi	*sdravo*	's-dra-vo'
goodbye	*nasvidenje*	'nas-vee-den-yeh'
bye	*adijo*	'ah-dee-yo'
thank you	*hvala*	'h-vah-la'
thank you very much	*hvala lepa*	'h-vah-la lay-pah'

Numbers

English	Slovenian	Pronounced
one	ena	'ay-nah'
two	dve	'd-veh'
three	tri	'tree'
four	štiri	'shtee-ree'
five	pet	'pet'
six	šest	'shest'
seven	sedem	'seh-dem'
eight	osem	'o-sem'
nine	devet	'day-vet'
ten	deset	'day-set'

Food and drink

English	Slovenian	Pronounced
beef	govedina	'goh-veh-deena'
beer	pivo	'pee-vo'
bread	kruh	'kruch' (with the Scottish 'ch')
cheese	sir	'seer'
chicken	piščanec	'peesh-chan-ets'
coffee (an espresso)	...kava	'car-vah'
...with milk	z mlekom	'z m-lek-om'
with cream	s smetano	's smet-ah-no'
egg	jajce	'yait-say'
fish	ribe	'ree-beh'
milk	mleko	'm-lek-oh'
onion	čebula	'cheh-boo-lah'
potato	krompir	'krom-peer'
sandwich	sendvič	'send-veech'
soup	juha	'you-ha'

English	Slovenian	Pronounced
tea	čaj	'chai'
black tea	črni čaj	'chair-nee chai'
trout	postrv	'pos-tru'
vegetables	zelenjava	'ze-len-ya-vah'
water	voda	'voh-da'
sparkling	radenska	'rah-den-skah'
wine	vino	'vee-no' (the stress on the last syllable)
red wine	rdeče vino	'r-dech-eh vee-no'
white wine	belo vino	'bay-low vee-no'

Other useful words

English	Slovenian	Pronounced
cave	jama	'ya-mah'
cycling	kolesarske	'kol-es-ar-skay'
forest	gozd	'goz-d'
inner tube	zračnico	'z-ratch-neets-oh'
meadow	travnik	'trau-neek'
mountain	planinska	'pla-neen-skah'
puncture	punkcija	'punk-tsee-ya'
repair	popraviti	'pop-ra-vee-tee'
river	reka	'ray-ka'
trail	pot	'pot'
workshop	delavnica	'day-lau-neets-ah'

Appendix B
Accommodation

Slovenia depends on tourism for a good portion of its income. As a consequence, there is a fine range of accommodation on offer. A good place to start looking for somewhere to stay would be a comparison website. There are any number of these of course, however, when looking for hotels I generally use Hotels. com (hotels.com), which has a wide range of options, often discounted, and gives you one free night for every 10 nights paid for.

Nowadays, many people like to use Airbnb (www.airbnb.co.uk). This is a website that puts you directly in contact with thousands of privately owned accommodation options. Particularly useful if you're on a budget, you can set what kind of place you're looking for and choose anything from rooms in the owner's house to private apartments or whole cottages.

Finally, an excellent Slovenia-only website for finding accommodation (and a good deal else as well) is Slotrips (www.slovenia-trips. com/eng/accomodation). Run by a biking fan, this has the full range of sleeping options from camping and hostels to tourist farms and spas.

For a few, more specific recommendations, please see the different regions below.

Gorenjska

Budget
Hostel Pod Voglom
Ribčev Laz 60
4265 Bohinjsko jezero
tel +386 4 572 34 61
www.hostel-podvoglom.com/en

This hostel provides a friendly welcome right on the shores of Lake Bohinj. It has some bike cleaning facilities and, if you book ahead, you can have basic but hearty food in the evenings.

Hostel Barovc
Naselje Ivana Krivca 22
4280 Kranjska Gora
tel +386 4 582 04 00
hostel-barovc.com/en

This hostel does sit a short walk outside of the centre of Kranjska Gora, but it's clean and friendly and does have its own bar and serves food.

Camp Danica
Naselje Ivana Krivca 22
4280 Kranjska Gora
tel +386 4 582 04 00
www.camp-danica.si/en

Danica camp ground sits right next to the beautiful Sava River as it flows away from Lake Bohinj. The site has excellent camping facilities and is just outside the town of Bohinjska Bistrica, with all necessary services. The camp also sits on Route 1.

Mid-range
Penzion Berc
Pod Stražo 13
4260 Bled
tel +386 4 576 56 58
www.berc-sp.si/en

A relaxed and traditional Slovenian inn, Berc has what may be some of the best dining in Bled.

Penzion Livada
Koroška ulica 24
4280 Kranjska Gora
tel +386 4 171 90 21
www.penzion-livada.si/en

Located right in the centre of town, this clean and pleasant alpine guesthouse also does good food.

River Cottage – Hiša ob potoku
Kurirska pot 13
4281 Mojstrana
Slovenia
tel +386 (0) 40 782433
tel +386 (0) 40 691677
www.rivercottageslovenia.com

High end

Grand Hotel Toplice
Cesta svobode 12
4260 Bled
tel +386 4 579 16 00
www.sava-hotels-resorts.com/en

The only five-star hotel in Bled, this glorious reminder of Hapsburg glories is still the best (and most expensive) place to stay in the town.

Hotel Park
Cankarjeva cesta 15
4260 Bled
tel +386 4 579 18 00
www.sava-hotels-resorts.com/en

Right by the lake in Bled, this newly refurbished hotel has great views and lovely facilities, including a roof-top pool.

Hotel Lek
Vršiška cesta 38
4280 Kranjska Gora
tel +386 4 588 15 20
www.hotel-lek.si

This lovely alpine hotel sits just a short walk from the centre of Kranjska Gora and offers good dining and excellent facilities for relaxation.

The Soča Valley

Budget

Hotel Lucija
Most na Soči 57
5216 Most na Soči
tel +386 5 381 32 90
www.hotel-lucija.com

This hotel is great value and, whilst being very comfortable, definitely counts as budget. It's also a *kolesarska* hotel, which means it has facilities for cyclists.

Hostel Soča Rocks
Mala vas 120
5230 Bovec
tel +386 4 131 77 77
hostelsocarocks.com

If you like a party atmosphere at your accommodation, then Soča Rocks might be the place for you. It's within spitting distance of the bars and restaurants of Bovec and they hire out bikes as well as offering discounts on other activities.

Kamp Koren
Ladra 1b
5222 Kobarid
tel +386 5 389 13 11
www.kamp-koren.si/en

Situated on the edge of Kobarid in the middle of the Soča Valley, Kamp Koren has facilities for tents and campervans as well as having eco-chalets. It hires out mountain bikes and, at the end of the day, you can relax with a beer right next to the famous River Soča.

Mid-range

Hotel Ana
Žaga 156a
5224 Srpenica
tel +386 5 384 55 12
www.hotel-ana.com/en

There isn't much around Hotel Ana (apart from mountains and the stunning River Soča, of course) because it's a little way outside of Bovec. However, it has a restaurant and bar and, importantly, offers bike hire and servicing.

Apartmaji Mavrič
Dvor 61
5230 Bovec
tel +386 4 055 98 82
www.apartments-mavric.com/en

This small collection of privately owned apartments sits just on the edge of Bovec but within walking distance of the bars and restaurants. Owned and run by Bostjan, who is a keen biker himself, they have a bike store and facilities for repairs and information about biking.

Penzion Šterk
Most na Soči 55
5216 Most na Soči
tel +386 5 388 70 65
www.penzion-sterk.si/en

Situated at the confluence between two rivers in Most na Soči, this excellent restaurant also has very pleasant rooms. If you want to be away from the tourist hubbub further up the Soča Valley then look no further.

Hemingway House
Volaričeva ulica 10
5222 Kobarid
tel +386 4 077 41 06
www.hemingwayhouseslovenia.com

This B&B is located in an historic house in the centre of Kobarid. Each of the rooms is an apartment and they're beautifully decorated.

High end
Hotel Hvala
Trg svobode 1
5222 Kobarid
tel +386 5 389 93 00
www.hotelhvala.si/en

This comfortable hotel sits right in the town centre of Kobarid. It also contains one of the best restaurants in town so, apart from biking, you need never leave.

The South
Budget
Hostel Situla
Dilančeva ulica 1
8000 Novo mesto
tel +386 7 394 20 00
www.situla.si/en

Located in an historic building right in the old town centre of Novo Mesto, you're unlikely to find a more attractive hostel anywhere. Good restaurant and bar attached.

Hostel Ajdovščina
Cesta IV. Prekmorske 61a
5270 Ajdovščina
tel +386 5 368 93 83
www.youth-hostel.si

A part of Hostelling International, this conveniently located hostel has four blue triangles and is a modern, comfortable place to stay.

Camping Pivka Jama
Veliki Otok 50
6230 Postojna
tel +386 5 720 39 93
camping-postojna.com/en

A beautiful campsite set into the woods just outside Postojna, Pivka Jama has facilities for tents, campervans and rents out bungalows. There are a plethora of sporting facilities, a good restaurant and even its own cave.

Mid-range
Hotel Gold Club
Goriška cesta 25
5270 Ajdovščina
tel +386 5 364 47 00
www.hotelgoldclub.eu/en

It may have an interesting name but Hotel Gold Club is a stylish and pleasant place to stay if you're basing yourself in Ajdovščina. Good restaurant on site too.

Hotel Sport
Kolodvorska ulica 1
Postojna
tel +386 5 720 22 44
www.sport.hostel.com

Its interiors may be a bit dated nowadays but Hotel Sport is a clean, comfortable and well looked-after hotel. Most important of all, however, is that it is dedicated to the needs of cyclists of every stripe.

Apartment Homovec
Predgriže 39
5274 Lome
www.booking.com
(search 'Apartment Homovec')

If you fancy self-catering and you like a quiet life, you couldn't do better than this family-run apartment near to Črni Vrh. Owned by sports fanatics, there is plenty of information available on biking.

High end
Vitarium Hotel
Šmarješke Toplice 100
8220 Šmarješke Toplice
tel +386 8 205 03 00
www.terme-krka.com/us/en/destinations/

A large and luxurious spa resort set in beautiful woodland not far from the two rides at Doljenske Toplice. The facilities are great and there's a member of staff who can give advice on riding. The Terme Krka website also has cheaper options in the area.

Hotel Jama
Jamska cesta 30
6230 Postojna
tel +386 5 700 01 03
www.postojnska-jama.eu/en/
get-to-know-the-park/overnight-stay

Situated next to the world-famous Postojna Cave, this Socialist-era hotel is rather unprepossessing from the outside. Inside, however, there has been a spectacular renovation in recent years and this is now one of the nicest places to stay in the area.

Central and North East

Budget

Ecohotel Koroš
Jamnica 10
2391 Prevalje
tel +386 2 870 30 60
www.bikenomad.com

Probably the finest MTB accommodation is Slovenia. A five-bike awarded *kolesarski* hostel, they have every facility you could need – including their own mountain bike trail. Located near to Črna na Koroškem.

Hostel Uni
Volkmerjev prehod 7
2000 Maribor
tel +386 2 250 67 00
www.youth-hostel.si

Right in the heart of Maribor's old town, this International Hostelling hostel has the highest rating for accommodation.

Kamp Resnik
Nevlje 1a
1240 Kamnik
tel +386 1 831 73 14
kampresnik.com

Camp Resnik is just a short walk from Kamnik and it's a little green haven for campers and campervans alike.

Mid-range

Golte
Radegunda 19C
3330 Mozirje
tel +386 3 839 11 00
www.golte.si/eng

High in the mountains, Golte is an adrenalin junky's dream. There is bike hire, storage and wash facilities and loads of other activities for those of an adventurous nature.

Hotel Bellevue
Na Slemenu 35
2208 Pohorje
tel +386 2 607 51 00
www.hotelbellevue.si/en

This hill-top hotel with spectacular views is surprisingly good value. It's right at the top of the downhill park and offers bike and cleaning facilities as well as advice on rides.

Terme Snovik
Snovik 7
1219 Laze v Tuhinju
tel +386 1 834 41 00
terme-snovik.si/en

Snovik is not far from Kamnik and sits up in the mountains. It's a good spot for relaxation and has plenty for families.

Pri Cesarju
Tunjiška 1
1240 Kamnik
tel +386 4 162 98 46
pricesarju.si/en

This is a lovely and historic B&B located in the centre of Kamnik. Expect a friendly welcome and an elegant stay.

High end

Hotel Habakuk
Pohorska ulica 59
2000 Maribor
tel +386 2 300 81 00
www.hotel-habakuk.si/en

Sitting right at the bottom of the World Downhill route, Habakuk is a spa resort with a fabulous pool and recreational facilities.

Appendix C
Useful information

Medical facilities
The European emergency number is 112. Use this number in any emergency situation. The call is free and can be used with phones that are roaming.

Gorenjska
Bled
Mladinska cesta 1
4260 Bled
tel +386 4 575 40 00

Bohinjska Bistrica
Triglavska cesta 15
4264 Boh. Bistrica
tel +386 4 572 71 00

Kranj
Gosposvetska ulica 10
tel +386 4 208 20 20

Kranjska Gora
Koroška ulica 2
4280 Kranjska Gora
tel +386 4 588 46 00

Soča
Bovec
Kot 48
tel +386 5 388 60 57

Kobarid
Trg svobode 3A
tel +386 5 388 11 20

Tolmin
Prešernova ulica 6
tel +386 5 388 11 20

The South
Ajdovščina
Tovarniška cesta 3
tel +386 5 369 30 00

Logatec
Notranjska cesta 2
1370 Logatec
tel +386 1 750 82 29

Novo Mesto
Kandijska cesta 4
8000 Novo mesto
tel +386 7 391 67 00

Postojna
Prečna ulica 2
tel +386 5 726 54 01

Vipava
Beblerjeva ulica 5
tel +386 5 365 51 10

Central and North East
Celje
Gregorčičeva 5
tel +386 3 543 40 00

Črna na Koroškem
Center 144a
2393 Črna na Koroškem
tel +386 2 870 41 11

Kamnik
Novi trg 26
tel +386 1 830 86 00

Maribor
Ulica Talcev 9, 2000 Maribor
tel +386 2 228 62 00

Trbovlje
Rudarska cesta 9
1420 Trbovlje
tel +386 3 562 63 22

Tourist information centres
The tourist information centres in Slovenia are excellent. The staff will speak English; they will have maps to sell and, quite possibly, biking-specific maps for free.

Gorenjska
Bled
Cesta svobode 10
4260 Bled
tel +386 4 574 11 22
tdbled@telemach.net

Bohinjska Bistrica
Triglavska cesta 30
4265 Bohinjska Bistrica
tel +386 4 574 75 90
info@bohinj.si
www.bohinj.si

Kranj
Glavni trg 2
tel +386 4 238 04 50
tic@tourism-kranj.si
www.tourism-kranj.si

Kranjska Gora
Tičarjeva 2
4280 Kranjska Gora
tel +386 4 580 94 40
tic@kranjska-gora.eu
www.kranjska-gora.si

Soča
Bovec
Trg golobarskih žrtev 8
tel +386 5 389 64 44
info@bovec.si
www.bovec.si

Kobarid
Trg svobode 16
5222 Kobarid
tel +386 5 380 04 90
www.visit-soca.com

Tolmin
Petra Skalarja 4
tel +386 5 380 04 80
www.visit-soca.com

The South
Ajdovščina
Cesta IV. prekomorske 61a
5270 Ajdovščina
tel +386 5 365 91 40
www.tic-ajdovscina.si

Logatec
Tržaška cesta 50 A
tel +386 1 759 07 00
obcina.logatec@logatec.si
www.logatec.si

Novo Mesto
Glavni trg 6
8000 Novo mesto
tel +386 7 393 92 63
tic@novomesto.si
www.visitnovomesto.si

Postojna
Ljubljanska cesta 4
6230 Postojna
tel +386 5 728 07 88
vlasta.kolenc@postojna.si
www.postojna.si

Vipava
Glavni trg 1
tel +386 5 364 70 41
tic.vipava@siol.net
www.izvirna-vipavska.si

Central and North East
Celje
Krekov trg 3
tel +386 3 428 79 36;
+386 3 492 50 81
tic@celje.si
www.celeia.info

Črna na Koroškem
Center 100
tel +386 2 823 82 69
pkm@siol.net
www.crna.si

Kamnik
Glavni trg 2
tel +386 1 831 82 50
info@kamnik.si
www.kamnik-tourism.si

Maribor
Partizanska cesta 6a
2000 Maribor
tel +386 2 234 66 11
zzt@maribor.si
www.maribor-pohorje.si

Trbovlje
Ulica 1. junija 4
1420 Trbovlje
tel +386 3 562 25 51

Bike hire/repair

Gorenjska
Bled
3Glav Adventures
Ljubljanska cesta 1
4260 Bled
tel +386 4 168 31 84
www.3glav.com

Bohinjska Bistrica
Destina
Prečna ulica 1B
4264 Bohinjska Bistrica
tel +386 4 574 70 22
tina@destina.si
www.destina.si/en/rent-a-bike

Kranjska Gora
MTB Republic
Borovška cesta 102A
4280 Kranjska Gora
tel +386 3 127 20 88
www.bikerental.si/en

Soča
Bovec
Soča Rafting
Trg golobarskih žrtev 14
5230 Bovec
tel +386 5 389 62 00
info@socarafting.si
www.socarafting.si/eng

Kobarid
X Point
Trg svobode 6
5222 Kobarid
tel +386 5 388 53 08
info@xpoint.sien.xpoint.si

Positive Sport
Trg svobode 13
5222 Kobarid
tel +386 4 065 44 75
info@positive-sport.com
positive-sport.com

The South
Novo Mesto
Šmarješke Toplice
Šmarješke Toplice 100
8220
tel +386 8 205 03 00
www.terme-krka.com/us/en/desinations

Postojna
Sport Hotel
Kolodvorska cesta 1
6230 Postojna
tel +386 5 720 22 44
info@sport-hotel.si
www.sport-hotel.si

Central and North East
Ravne na Koroškem
Ecohotel Koroš
Jamnica 10
2391 Prevalje
tel +386 2 870 30 60
info@bikenomad.com
www.bikenomad.com

Maribor
Bike Park Maribor
Pohorska ulica 60
2000 Maribor
tel +386 5 925 90 41
info@bikeparkpohorje.si
www.bikeparkpohorje.si/en

Other useful websites

Flights
EasyJet
www.easyjet.com

Wizzair
wizzair.com

Adria Airways
www.adria.si/en

Trains
International Rail
www.internationalrail.co.uk

Eurostar
www.eurostar.com/uk-en

Slovenia Železnice
www.slo-zeleznice.si/en

Buses
Bus Station Ljubljana
www.ap-ljubljana.si/en

DRD Turizem
www.drd.si/en and click on 'timetables'

Cars
Holiday Autos
www.holidayautos.com

and finally, for real emergencies...

British Embassy
Trg republike 3
1000 Ljubljana
tel +386 1 200 39 10
info@british-embassy.si

Listing of Cicerone Guides

BRITISH ISLES CHALLENGES, COLLECTIONS AND ACTIVITIES
The Book of the Bivvy
The Book of the Bothy
The End to End Trail
The Mountains of England and Wales: Vol 1 Wales
The Mountains of England and Wales: Vol 2 England
The National Trails
The UK's County Tops
Three Peaks, Ten Tors

UK CYCLING
20 Classic Sportive Rides in South East England
20 Classic Sportive Rides in South West England
Cycling in the Cotswolds
Cycling in the Hebrides
Cycling in the Lake District
Cycling in the Yorkshire Dales
Cycling the Pennine Bridleway
Mountain Biking in Southern and Central Scotland
Mountain Biking in the Lake District
Mountain Biking in the Yorkshire Dales
Mountain Biking in West and North West Scotland
Mountain Biking on the North Downs
Mountain Biking on the South Downs
The C2C Cycle Route
The End to End Cycle Route
The Lancashire Cycleway

SCOTLAND
Backpacker's Britain: Northern Scotland
Ben Nevis and Glen Coe
Great Mountain Days in Scotland
Not the West Highland Way Scotland
Scotland's Best Small Mountains
Scotland's Far West
Scotland's Mountain Ridges
Scrambles in Lochaber
The Ayrshire and Arran Coastal Paths
The Border Country
The Cape Wrath Trail
The Great Glen Way
The Great Glen Way Map Booklet
The Hebrides
The Isle of Mull
The Isle of Skye
The Skye Trail
The Southern Upland Way

The Speyside Way
The Speyside Way Map Booklet
The West Highland Way
Walking Highland Perthshire
Walking in Scotland's Far North
Walking in the Angus Glens
Walking in the Cairngorms
Walking in the Ochils, Campsie Fells and Lomond Hills
Walking in the Pentland Hills
Walking in the Southern Uplands
Walking in Torridon
Walking Loch Lomond and the Trossachs
Walking on Arran
Walking on Harris and Lewis
Walking on Jura, Islay and Colonsay
Walking on Rum and the Small Isles
Walking on the Orkney and Shetland Isles
Walking on Uist and Barra
Walking the Corbetts Vol 1 South of the Great Glen
Walking the Corbetts Vol 2 North of the Great Glen
Walking the Galloway Hills
Walking the Munros Vol 1 – Southern, Central and Western Highlands
Walking the Munros Vol 2 – Northern Highlands and the Cairngorms
West Highland Way Map Booklet
Winter Climbs Ben Nevis and Glen Coe
Winter Climbs in the Cairngorms

NORTHERN ENGLAND TRAILS
A Northern Coast to Coast Walk
Hadrian's Wall Path
Hadrian's Wall Path Map Booklet
Pennine Way Map Booklet
The Coast to Coast Map Booklet
The Coast to Coast Walk
The Dales Way
The Pennine Way

NORTH EAST ENGLAND, YORKSHIRE DALES AND PENNINES
Great Mountain Days in the Pennines
Historic Walks in North Yorkshire
South Pennine Walks
St Oswald's Way and St Cuthbert's Way
The Cleveland Way and the Yorkshire Wolds Way
The Cleveland Way Map Booklet

The North York Moors
The Reivers Way
The Teesdale Way
The Yorkshire Dales: South and West
Walking in County Durham
Walking in Northumberland
Walking in the North Pennines
Walking in the Yorkshire Dales: North and East
Walking in the Yorkshire Dales: South and West
Walks in Dales Country
Walks in the Yorkshire Dales

NORTH WEST ENGLAND AND THE ISLE OF MAN
Historic Walks in Cheshire
Isle of Man Coastal Path
The Lune Valley and Howgills – A Walking Guide
The Ribble Way
Walking in Cumbria's Eden Valley
Walking in Lancashire
Walking in the Forest of Bowland and Pendle
Walking on the Isle of Man
Walking on the West Pennine Moors
Walks in Lancashire Witch Country
Walks in Ribble Country
Walks in Silverdale and Arnside
Walks in the Forest of Bowland

LAKE DISTRICT
Great Mountain Days in the Lake District
Helvellyn
Lake District Winter Climbs
Lake District: High Level and Fell Walks
Lake District: Low Level and Lake Walks
Lakeland Fellranger
The Central Fells
The Far Eastern Fells
The Mid-Western Fells
The Near Eastern Fells
The Northern Fells
The North-Western Fells
The Southern Fells
The Western Fells

For full information on all our
guides, books and eBooks,
visit our website:
www.cicerone.co.uk

Walking – Trekking – Mountaineering – Climbing – Cycling

Over 40 years, Cicerone have built up an outstanding collection of over 300 guides, inspiring all sorts of amazing adventures.

Every guide comes from extensive exploration and research by our expert authors, all with a passion for their subjects. They are frequently praised, endorsed and used by clubs, instructors and outdoor organisations.

All our titles can now be bought as **e-books**, **ePubs** and **Kindle** files and we also have an online magazine – **Cicerone Extra** – with features to help cyclists, climbers, walkers and trekkers choose their next adventure, at home or abroad.

Our website shows any **new information** we've had in since a book was published. Please do let us know if you find anything has changed, so that we can publish the latest details. On our **website** you'll also find great ideas and lots of detailed information about what's inside every guide and you can buy **individual routes** from many of them online.

It's easy to keep in touch with what's going on at Cicerone by getting our monthly **free e-newsletter**, which is full of offers, competitions, up-to-date information and topical articles. You can subscribe on our home page and also follow us on **Facebook** and **Twitter** or dip into our **blog**.

Cicerone – the very best guides for exploring the world.

CICERONE

2 Police Square Milnthorpe Cumbria LA7 7PY
Tel: 015395 62069 info@cicerone.co.uk
www.cicerone.co.uk and **www.cicerone-extra.com**